PAUL, DURCAN'S diary

NEW
ISLAND

Paul Durcan's Diary
First published October 2003
by New Island
2 Brookside
Dundrum Road
Dublin 14
www.newisland.ie

The author has asserted his moral rights.

ISBN 1 904301 40 1

The lines from 'If Ever You Go To Dublin Town' by Patrick Kavanagh are reprinted by kind permission of the Trustees of the Estate of the late Katherine B. Kavanagh, through the Jonathan Williams Literary Agency.

The lines from 'For My Brother Reported Missing In Action' by Thomas Merton are reprinted by kind permission of New Directions Publishing Corporation through Pollinger Limited Authors' Agents.

British Library Cataloguing in Publication Data. A CIP catalogue record for this book is available from the British Library.

Typeset by New Island
Cover design by New Island
Cover photograph by Harry Pettis
Printed in the UK by Mackays of Chatham Ltd

New Island received financial assistance from The Arts Council
(An Chomhairle Ealaíon), Dublin, Ireland.

10 9 8 7 6 5 4 3

CONTENTS

TO CATRIONA CROWE
The Flaming Listener

Acknowledgements

These diary pieces were broadcast on *Today with Pat Kenny*, RTÉ Radio 1; the date at the end of each piece is the date of broadcast. My gratitude to one and all on the *Today with Pat Kenny* team: the producers, the editorial assistants and the sound technicians; Rachel Graham, Pat Costello, Conor Kavanagh, Pat Coyle, Cathal Portéir, Geraldine Collins, Mary Duffy, Joan Brady, Aoífe Nic Cormaic, Diarmuid Byrne, Muriel Carney, Síle Ní Bhaoil, Myles Neylon, Tom Nolan, Alex O'Gorman, Pat Ryan, Michael Wright and Noel Roberts. Pat Kenny made me welcome on his programme as did his deputy Leo Enright.

A special word of thanks to the series producer Marian Richardson, who also commissioned the series. I have had the good fortune to work with some of the outstanding practitioners of public service broadcasting in RTÉ Radio: Kieran Sheedy, John Skehan, Donal Flanagan, Dan Collins, Ed Mulhall, Peter Browne, Ann Walsh, Jacqui Corcoran, Julian Vignoles and, for the last three years, Marian Richardson.

Paul Durcan
June 16, 2003

Feast of the Epiphany 2001

Last Saturday, January 6, was the Feast of the Epiphany. I'd
been looking forward to it all week. Every night on my walk
around my quarter – Ringsend-Irishtown – I'd been keeping
an eye on the cribs in the windows of people's flats and
terraces, especially on one window in the heart of Ringsend
village where the Three Wise Kings had been actually knitted
– hand-knitted! Homely potentates in green wool and yellow
wool and red wool.

The day itself dawned bright and not too cold. In fact
Spring was in the trees as well as in the air as I walked across
Ringsend Park at 9.45 a.m. A blackbird was in full-throated
song at the Pigeon House Road gate and the bare boughs
had a red sheen. On the football pitches hundreds of birds
were having a good feed: on one pitch about thirty oyster-
catchers and, on the next pitch, about twenty Brent Geese
– our annual visitors from Greenland. A young man
walking past said 'Hallo'. On another day he might have
said 'Eff Off' but no, today he said 'Hallo'. And as for

broken bottles, there wasn't too much broken glass on the path.

In Ringsend Church all the lights were on and people were glowing, including even the mourners around the coffin of the old lady, Sheila, whose funeral was also about to take place. The young priest, too, exuded springtime: eager and brisk and cheerful and humorous and serious and quite obviously totally sincere and with a smile.

I walked back by the river and stared in amazement once again at one of those ginormous warehouse-container ships that looks like a vast crate floating in the middle of a raindrop and I wonder what it must be like to be sitting on top of it in the middle of the empty ocean.

Back in my cave I scan *The Irish Times* for news of the day that is in it, the Feast of the Epiphany, the greatest day of the year. But not a mention of it in the news pages. Even their Saturday religious column on the editorial page called 'Thinking Aloud' makes no reference to this historic and astonishing day. True, in their 'Weekend Review', they have an art-historical-literary piece on the Three Wise Kings but oddly it contains not a syllable on the Epiphany itself and odder still it winds up with a literary flourish referring us to Yeats's and Eliot's poems on the Magi but with no reference to the greatest twentieth-century literary writing in English on the Epiphany, the seventh chapter of Evelyn Waugh's novel *Helena*. Same in next day's Sunday papers: no mention of the Epiphany. Same on Monday.

Now I know how we're all supposed to be modern and post-modern and progressive and secular and highly sophisticated and Into the Internet and across the I.T. and that we have what we call separation of powers – that is, separation of Church and State. But surely there is separation and separation.

It seems to me that our state of affairs has gone far beyond anything you might call 'separation'. This is the two-faced life; and not only on a national scale but also on a global scale.

Only twelve days ago – twelve days ago! – we were all hopping and lepping about on Christmas Day. But Christmas Day of course is purely a Jewish day – that is, it's the day commemorating the birth of the Jewish holy man and faith-healer Jesus Christ to a Jewish family surrounded entirely by his Jewish community. And an amazing and beautiful spectacle it is – this great Jewish birthday. Pure Chagall, Xmas Trees and all.

But – and this is where it's at or where it used to be at until we progressed into our Higher Schizophrenia – it's another twelve days before those of us who are not Jews come into the picture. Those of us who are American Indians or Australian Aboriginals or English or Irish.

It's we outsiders who are not Jews who are the Three Wise Men – the Three Wise Kings – the Three Wise Pagans. We're the Three Guys or Gals who went by our own feelings – who trusted to our own intuitions – who followed our own noses instead of keeping up with the Joneses or the Saddam Husseins. And of course 'Kings' is just a nickname. It's because we're ordinary folk that they call us 'Kings'. I'm Melchior by the way and, as I say, I've lodgings in Ringsend and that's Caspar and he lives in Phibsborough – in Great Western Square, actually – and the third fellow with the mustard hair is Balthassar and he lives in Westport, Co. Mayo, in the Old Protestant Rectory.

So why then is the Epiphany such big news? Why should it have been on the front pages of the newspapers? And, anyway, what does it mean, that word 'Epiphany'? Poetry. An old word for poetry.

Meaning a glimpse of reality; just a glimpse of reality; enough of a glimpse to keep us going until the next day. And what is reality? Reality is all those tiny, infinitesimal details that go to make up ten seconds in your life or a minute or two. Which is why it should have been headlines last Saturday. Newspapers are supposed to put us in touch with reality.

In fact the top headline on the front page of last Saturday's *Irish Times* was: BURROWS MAY RUN AGAINST HICKEY FOR OCI POST. Now of course it is important who gets to run the Olympic Council of Ireland – definitely – but, still, in the scale of news values, does it rate with the Epiphany?

To call a spade a spade or a javelin a javelin, our current way of living in communal schizophrenia scares me. Living our lives in compartments. Religion, sport, art, work, all in their different sections. The Sports section, the Magazine section, the Weekend section, the News section. Is it any wonder that the world feels like such an insane place with all us poor patients being chased around by hatchet-faced newspaper policemen with haloes around their hatchets?

Still, it was a great day, the Feast of the Epiphany last Saturday; a glimpse of reality, a glimpse of the first real reconciliation of humans ever recorded in history when we pagans came in from the cold and celebrated the birth of a Jewish baby. At ten o'clock in Ringsend Church we brought the gift of a dead woman, Sheila, who had lived a long and good and faithful life. Is that not news?

O Joxer and I sez to myself, Joxer, I sez to myself, what is the news, Joxer, what is the news?

January 10, 2001

As I listen to yet another citizen badmouthing Celia Larkin and Bertie Ahern – all these Letters to the Editor and calls to the radio – I ask you: are we freeborn Irish really this mean, this hypocritical, this boorish?

I was once married myself and to a wonderful woman and we have two smashing daughters. Alas, bad luck hit us and we had to separate. It could happen to the Angel Gabriel. It could happen to you.

That was the worst time of my life – which won't come as any surprise to Bertie or Miriam Ahern or to any of you who have had the misfortune to see your marriage go on the rocks.

These days I live alone in a cave in the Dublin docklands. But my wife, I am glad to say, has a partner. They have been together now for at least twelve years.

Myself, I would have given anything to have got married again or to have had a permanent partner but no such luck has come my way. In this intolerant country it's not easy for a separated man or a separated woman to meet a new partner and harder still to meet a new spouse.

When I cry to God – as I do, being human – I ask forgiveness for my *un-natural* situation. It is totally *un-natural* and, therefore, wrong for a man or woman to have to live alone and to be isolated from all intimacy.

It is a terrible thing to be companionless, not to have someone to exist for.

Also, being separated, I know what it is like to be on the receiving end of badmouthing, malice, exclusion. Some of my own family treat me as a criminal or as a second-class citizen because I am separated. I have committed the crime of separation and, therefore, I am morally reprehensible and I am not entitled to first-class rights or normal courtesies.

If I was to count out for you all the professional and liberal – as well as conservative – people who have snubbed me because of my ex-marital status, we'd be here until Val Joyce, that courteous man, that civilised man, comes on at midnight and talks a bit of sense and sensibility to the nation.

So I envy as well as admire Bertie Ahern and Celia Larkin and I recognise the cruelty of those who badmouth them.

As for all this high-principled indignation about our Head of State and his 'being in an *irregular* relationship', such guff should be recognised for the sanctimonious hypocrisy which it is. People who badmouth Bertie and Celia – have you noticed that they all share certain vital statistics?

Here's a profile of your average Celia-hater:

- They're the sort who evaluate their fellow human beings in terms exclusively of money and property.

- As well as having pebbles in their shoes, they carry stones in their pockets.

- They are hysterical creatures.

- They take holidays twice a year: in Thailand and in the mansionette cottage in Donegal, which, of course, far from being a cottage, is a gorgeous pile of skylights and dormers on a heap of split-levels.

~ They are haters of art, literature, music. They boast about their ignorance but they are proud of their familiarity with muzak. They especially loathe architecture and can feel only at home in blocks of grim design and tasteless decor.

~ They are *addictive* churchgoers. They do not *choose* to go to Church; they go because it is a compulsive habit.

~ They employ language as a weapon to wound and they are big into legal and medical jargon. 'I hear *he* has a dodgy duodenal, and *she* is a born recidivist.'

~ They like to read of the misfortunes of other people. But when confronted with good, decent, ordinary citizens like Bertie and Celia, they pine for the rat poison of misfortune.

~ They are people with no manners; and to have no manners is to have sold your soul.

I salute Bertie Ahern – he'd do any country proud as Prime Minister – and I salute his partner Celia Larkin for her courage and dignity in the face of the boorish behaviour of some of her countrymen and countrywomen. We should be grateful to each of them for setting us such an open, honest, brave example.

And what a beautiful name she has – Celia Larkin!

Dear Boor, spit out your vile bile and relax and listen to that beautiful name come over the airwaves to you: 'Celia Larkin'.

What these hypocrites would like is for Bertie to be a hypocrite too. They'd much prefer the Taoiseach to be like many another world leader and for him to have a *mistress* (hypocrites hyperventilate on words like '*mistress*') and that

7

he'd have her salted away in a stash in Ballsbridge in a luxury fortress.

Many of the hypocrites themselves have extra-marital relationships but that's 'no problem, boy' because it's all on the quiet, 'don't you know?' What a perverse position hypocrisy is!

But no, Bertie's a Dub, a northsider, a decent man, and he is glad to stride out with his handsome partner. More power to his chin – and to Celia's elbow.

It's high tide in Dublin Bay, and on Sandymount Strand a little girl – she couldn't be more than three or three and a half – in a matching black and white hat and coat is kneeling on the edge of the path watching the ocean waves running towards her. She is enthralled by the energy and uniqueness of each wave. That is how we should look at one another: as the little girl looks at each wave of the sea in awe and claps her hands. That is how I look at Celia Larkin, and the more she is in the picture on State occasions the more I like it. God mind her and her partner.

January 17, 2001

LIAM LAWLOR

The only entirely innocent news*makers* are the news*casters*: a body of people of extraordinary patience and equanimity.

Last Monday night week on the *Six-One* news on RTÉ 1 TV, Bryan Dobson began with the announcement that Liam Lawlor TD had received a jail sentence and would be beginning his sentence on the Wednesday; and a *solemn* announcement it was: the Downing Street *solemnity* of 'This country is at war with Germany.'

Or it was as if an earthquake had occurred.

Actually an earthquake *had* occurred in San Salvador but that news was inserted between recurring *solemn* announcements that Liam Lawlor TD had been sent to jail. It was a funereal liturgy – this fifty-minute news bulletin with the dignified and eminent newscaster Bryan Dobson (along with the equally dignified and eminent Una O'Hagan) again and again and again repeating at intervals that Liam Lawlor TD had been sentenced to jail and that unless he appealed to the Supreme Court before 2 p.m. on

Wednesday he would be entering Mountjoy Prison at 2 p.m. on Wednesday.

Why the *solemnity* of this liturgy? What can the news *choreographers* of this world be thinking about? Why are our news*casters* and, therefore, us the viewers by extension (for we viewers are the umbilically tied babies in the womb of the Tube) – why are we all put through such hoops, such straitjackets? Why cannot a thing be reported straight like it is?

Would it not have been more natural and, therefore, more humane – more *open* and *transparent* and *accountable* – for the news*caster* to have made the announcement splitting his sides laughing?

(Uproarious laughter) 'Mr Liam Lawlor has been sentenced to jail.' And for the newscaster, then, to introduce us to his interviewees Ruairí Quinn and Alan Shatter and, with the TV station having invited along some of Liam Lawlor's other critics and Bryan Dobson having jovially introduced us to these moral celebrities, then for a studio assistant to have opened the champagne or the stout or the whatever-you're-having-yourself and for them all to have joined in a warm-blooded, full-throated toast to the jailing of Liam Lawlor TD – the very contrary of gloating or solemnity.

I am not joking. I am absolutely not joking. I have been thinking about this all my life. About: THE NEWS. My father all his life listened to and/or watched THE NEWS; all my life I have listened to and/or watched THE NEWS.

On the Wednesday last week – Wednesday 17 – the news choreographers of Ireland were on tenterhooks to see if Liam Lawlor TD would appeal before 2 p.m. or go to jail. That afternoon I phoned a colleague and I asked her: 'What happened to our poor friend?'

'Who do you mean?'

'Our friend in West Dublin.'

'Liamo's in the clink,' she said.

I said 'That's my worst nightmare.'

'WHAT? That Liam Lawlor would be sent to prison? You can't be serious?'

'No – that I – I myself – would end up in prison.'

Yes. That *I* would end up in prison. That *anyone* would end up in prison. Next day, Thursday 18, the *Six-One* news briefly reported that a nineteen-year-old boy, John Wade of Tallaght, imprisoned also in Mountjoy the previous day, had been found dead in his cell; cause of death unknown; a death that on the Friday went unreported in *The Irish Times*, 'the Paper of Record'. Naturally everyone is saddened. But how would everyone feel if Liam Lawlor TD had been found dead in his cell? Would there have been grief? Or happiness? Or would it have been crocodile grief spiced with moral high-groundery?

I recollect when my daughter Síabhra was six or seven years old, one night in the bathroom in the basement of our home, Number Eleven, she suddenly saw the biggest, blackest spider you have ever seen and, in that moment, I have never seen such terror on another human being's face except on my own face when in the night I wake up in terror and humiliation seeing myself being led into a prison cell and the door being locked behind me. There are many things I fear in this life but my greatest fear, greater than the fear of death itself, is of being sent to prison.

When I was six years old my father was appointed a judge of the Circuit Court. From that day on, prison became a twenty-four-hour reality in my home. I used attend the trials at which my father was judge and I knew how much he dreaded sending a fellow human being to jail (except when confronted with dedicated evil) and how he would do anything within his power to give the lesser sentence and to mitigate the barbarity of the Irish penal system.

I remember too in a country town seeing an innocent young man, found guilty of manslaughter after a week in the dock, standing on the steps of the courthouse with his hands in handcuffs and his widowed mother weeping and the lawyers gravely huddling and the prison van waiting to snatch him; and the crowds of onlookers and so many of them relishing the spectacle, the greed of cruelty glittering all over their faces.

But my father too had his part in the play and he had to do his duty – as Liam Lawlor TD after being sentenced so simply put it: 'the judge has *his* job to do' – and week in, week out, year in, year out, my father committed people to the terrible prisons of Ireland and he himself grew sadder and sadder – and sadder and sadder still. The toll darkened his soul.

So all my life I have never passed Mountjoy Jail or Portlaoise or Limerick or Cork prisons without always feeling sad, so sad, sometimes suicidal.

This afternoon Liam Lawlor will be released from Mountjoy Jail, and of course it will be headlines on the *Six-One* news tonight, but I can only *hope* that just as there should have been a champagne party on the newscast the day he was sentenced, so tonight – with or without pictures of Liam Lawlor being released from jail – I can only *hope* that the champagne guests of last week will be back in studio but this time drowning their sorrows – in *openness* and *transparency* and *accountability* – sobbing and weeping at the sight of Liam Lawlor being let out of prison.

For why cannot a thing be reported straight like it is?

I am not joking.

January 24, 2001

LITTER CLAMPERS

Flying back into Dublin Airport I relish always that feeling of homecoming, of coming home to your own country even when you have no one to meet you and you have to stagger about in the dark searching the long-term car-park for your car and drive off to the twenty-four-hour to get bread and milk.

But next morning it's business as usual or, I should say, litter as usual. I am lucky to have some good neighbours but I think we'd all agree that there are days on the terrace when you have to tiptoe through crisp bags and sweet wrappers. Some say that the litter is 'blowing in the wind' but surely that's taking Bob Dylan a bit too far.

In Ringsend Park the one valiant Park Ranger, with the support of our brave local Green TD John Gormley, fights a hopeless battle with beer cans and broken bottles and burnt-out shrubs. Scorched earth is the new fashion in Ringsend this year; last year it was sawn-down trees. Great Balls of Fire

– as well as Great Balls of Litter. As you trek daily through the park, a body loses heart.

So on one of those really fresh sunny days we've been having – those batch loaves of January sunlight we have had – I lifted myself up by the laces of my Nike trainers and went for a walk on the beach at Merrion Gates where the Merrion Road ends and the Rock Road begins. I reckon it's thirty years since I last set foot on the beach at Merrion Gates. Which is a very odd thing to report since it's not much more than a mile away from where I live and I'm a regular half-power walker on Sandymount Strand which abuts on Merrion Gates.

Why the little interval of thirty years? Maybe because that end of Sandymount Strand is the Top End where the rich live and, as Hemingway said to Mary Colum, 'the rich are different from us' and Mary Colum replied 'Yes, they've more money than we do.'

So I'm walking along the secluded strand at Merrion Gates, a little haven on Dublin Bay where I toddled when I was a toddler in the pristine. Today couldn't be a more pleasant day and the tide so far out you'd think you could walk across the sands to Howth and have afternoon tea with the Princess of Baily. Hundreds of oyster-catchers feeding in the channels and red-legged shanks a-skittering.

And immediately at my feet the most wonderful display of litter you have ever set eyes on. A famous installation artist in the Irish Museum of Modern Art in Kilmainham – a Betsy Carter or a Karatoshi Megasaki – would be hard put to assemble and install such a galaxy of litter. And it's not exotic litter from across the seas – alas, no, we're not being made privy to the sewage secrets of Liverpool or Holyhead – no, it's ordinary, humdrum, home-grown Dublin litter. But a galaxy all the same – in the volume as well as quality of the litter. A darlin' little beach, a darlin' little beach.

Plastic bottles, plastic cans, plastic wrappers, plastic

detergent containers, plastic petrol containers, plastic cups – a paradise of plastic, dear boy. And bits of old footballs, tyres, traffic cones, hairy doormats, biros, yoghurt cartons, cigarette packets, glass bottles, paint tins, Tayto bags, shoes, trainers and one bright yellow Wellington boot to give one last painterly Turneresque touch to this seaside idyll. And all of these items laid out or piled or just scattered on beds of seashells.

And – it's much the same all over Ireland, isn't it, let's face it.

As I stand at noon on the beach at Merrion Gates in the sunlight pouring out its beatitudes on all this filth of litter, I think of one night in Tokyo two years ago. Two of us were chatting on a street corner and as we chatted I was aware of thirty or forty young people sitting on the steps of a building across the street. Maybe an hour passed and we were still talking when I noticed the crowd breaking up and as they drifted away two among them began collecting all the cans and bags, butts and gum which had accumulated while they'd been socialising.

I was astonished. I blurted 'What are they doing?'

My friend said 'Whadya mean – what are they doing? They're collecting all their own litter. Can't you see?'

'Yes of course I can see,' I said, 'but it's pretty odd, isn't it?'

'No. Not in Japan. In Japan, that's what everybody does, it's the way the Japanese are.'

Two weeks later on the Japanese Airlines flight back to London I found myself watching the highlights of that year's World Cup in Paris. And there was the Japanese team getting beaten and maybe ten thousand of their supporters sitting on, disconsolately, in the stands. And then they were standing up and exiting the stadium, simultaneously scurrying around picking up all their litter.

Well, obviously, the Japanese are different from the Irish, and the Japanese family has a different way of bringing up children. The Japanese are mostly all pagans and the Irish are mostly all Christians. But we're all humans who were once

15

monkeys, so surely we could bridge the gap or, at least, the litter gap.

But apart from family nurture and education, is there any more immediate solution to Ireland's litter psychosis?

Clamping. What? Clamping. Clamping is the only thing that has ever worked in Ireland. But that's cars. With litter, what is there to clamp?

You'd clamp the person who did the littering. You would not cause the person injury. You would use iron clamps with foam-rubber or velveteen lining. The person would be clamped for a minimum of two hours for spitting or casting chewing-gum on the footpath and a maximum of seven hours for throwing lighted cigarette butts out of motorcars. The clamped person would be provided with a portable loo and a telephone directory.

And/or: you'd clamp to the head of the offender a day-glo pink headband with one three-foot-high black feather attached and a built-in timer.

The clampers would carry out their work with the same efficiency and speed as they do with motorists. We'd have six Litter Clamper Vans touring Dublin city twenty-four hours day and night and a Litter Shop on Bachelor Quay next door to The Parking Shop.

There's only one alternative to clamping and that's to parachute into every city and town in Ireland two thousand Japanese in yellow boiler suits and white helmets who would give the ould countree the once over. The *once* over. Please Mr Dempsey, Mr Dempsey please. Please listen to me, please. The litter of Ireland is driving me insane. You're a clean-living Meath man and you're a logical Meath man and you're a Meath can-do man.

Konichiwa Dempsey-san, konichiwa, please us all a favour. It's 2001 AD – time crawl out filth – Ireland no more litter once for all. Arigato. Arigato. Dempsey-san.

January 31, 2001

ARCHBISHOP CONNELL BECOMES CARDINAL

When it was announced that Archbishop Connell of Dublin was to be made a Cardinal of the Roman Catholic Church the editorials next morning in our two national newspapers, the *Irish Independent* and *The Irish Times*, reversed their traditional roles.

Both newspapers congratulated Archbishop Connell and complimented him on being such a nice man. The sole hint of reservation came from the traditionally Roman Catholic *Irish Independent* whereas the traditionally more pro-testant *Irish Times* not only offered no dissent but also it performed curtseys as in a *Daily Telegraph* editorial in the 1950s complimenting the Queen on her latest tour of Africa. Our great pro-testant ancestors Burke and Goldsmith, Berkeley and Swift, Emmet and Tone and all the Yeats's must have blinked in their skulls.

The *Irish Independent*, on the other hand, in the last paragraph of its editorial headed 'Our New Cardinal', implied a reservation: 'Now we rejoice at the archbishop's elevation but when the time comes for his retirement we will need a successor with a gift for communication.'

The *Independent* was hinting that Archbishop Connell lacks a gift for communication. Does he? Archbishop Connell has clearly communicated the fact that not only is there nothing wrong with being a conservative but also that there are values worth conserving.

Furthermore, Archbishop Connell has always been out of step with political correctness and that in itself, in the context of our climate of suffocating political correctness, is refreshing.

The announcement was made last Sunday fortnight, January 21, which was designated 'Church Unity Sunday' as well as being the Third Sunday in Ordinary Time.

The readings of the day – the liturgical texts – were on the theme of what it means to be an evangelist: what it means to be a spiritual leader, an archbishop, a cardinal.

The First Reading was from the prophet Nehemiah in which Ezra the scribe and priest elucidates the importance of the Sabbath Day. 'Go, eat the fat, drink the sweet wine, and send a portion to the man who has nothing prepared ready. For this day is sacred to our Lord. Do not be sad: the joy of the Lord is your stronghold.'

The Second Reading was from the first letter of St Paul to the Corinthians in which he writes about the human anatomy: 'it is the least honourable parts of the body that we clothe with the greatest care'.

The Gospel Reading was Luke, Chapter 1, in which he tells why he decided to write his gospel. He felt an 'orderly' account was lacking.

In the Archdiocese of Dublin Sunday Mass Leaflet that day, published in his name and with his imprimatur '*cum permissu* Desmond Archbishop of Dublin', the Archbishop in his introductory note instructed us: 'We come together on Sunday to *listen* to the scriptures and to have them *explained*.'

The atmosphere and intention of this instruction is pure

Connellesque to anyone who has followed his statements down the last thirty years. Its requirement of passivity and its emphasis on logic are characteristic of Dr Connell's pre-Vatican-Two view of the world.

For myself, I do not believe that the mystery of life can be *explained*. With the mystery of life you can only respond existentially to the day that is in it and creatively through your conscience and your imagination working together. Such is the language of the Gospels which is the language of poetry, not of logic.

As for listening – of course. Yet listening is but one aspect of the Sabbath. One needs to meditate and celebrate and dream and play and smile as well as to listen.

Therefore, the most important thing to understand about Archbishop Connell is that he is, by his own choice, not a man of his time. He chose a very long time ago, as far back as the time when he was appointed Lecturer in Metaphysics in UCD in 1953, to reject twentieth-century existentialist philosophers and theologians and to retreat exclusively into medieval philosophy. It has taken great tenacity on his part to maintain this medieval position but it must seem odd to him to find *The Irish Times* endorsing him so obediently.

Odder still is that in his thirteen years as Archbishop he not only did not appoint John Moriarty as an advisor but also did not quote Moriarty in his sermons and letters. John Moriarty is Ireland's most outstanding philosopher-theologian since Bishop Berkeley in the eighteenth century, and back in the early 1960s in UCD he was Archbishop Connell's most brilliant student.

When he was appointed Archbishop in 1988, Archbishop Connell proposed to preach medieval doctrines on every subject: on family planning, on abortion, on homosexuality, on ecumenism, on women priests and on the integrity of the Sabbath Day.

I wish that Archbishop Connell had put into his cautious

defence of the Sabbath Day some of the fierce energy he has put into his anti-ecumenism and his sexuality pronouncements. The Sabbath Day has now largely gone missing in Dublin life with far more catastrophic consequences than contraception or ecumenism.

I can never forget the day that Archbishop Connell rebuked President McAleese for using the phrase 'sister churches'. On September 25 last year President McAleese at the National Conference of Priests stated: 'We can all sense disappointment and impatience on many fronts – the mixed messages about ecumenical dialogue with sister Christian churches.' On October 11 Dr Connell stated: 'The Catholic Church cannot be the sister church of any other church. She is the mother church.' On October 15 he delivered the *coup de grâce* to President McAleese when he quoted a whole passage verbatim from her speech and condemned it without once citing her name. If that was not fierce as well as scholastic swordplay, pray, what is?

I tiptoe around the ghostly autumn of 1997 when he rebuked the President for partaking of the Eucharist at a Church of Ireland service.

I pass by also the grief he has caused not only by his doctrines on homosexuality and women priests but also by the harshness with which he has expressed himself. How, I wonder, does he comport himself in the company of homosexual archbishops or women drivers?

Appalled by destitution, I wilt in the face of Dr Connell's wintry tones. I cry out to him as our Cardinal to give us a church of mercy, not an army of propaganda.

There is no more intolerant person than the rancorous liberal who expresses, say, a pro-abortion view but who will not courteously tolerate a different point of view. But equal to the rancorous liberal is the harsh conservative.

It would be churlish not to wish well the Phibsborough boy who is about to become a Cardinal but I implore him, even at this late-ish stage in his life, to think again about the rectitude of his rebukes of our President when she spoke of 'sister churches' in the context of our sectarian-sick country and when she partook of the Eucharist in the Church of Ireland. I implore him to recollect also that while the word 'obedience' occurs eighty-seven times in The New Testament, it is a word never once used by Christ.

I would implore him also to re-think his own phrase 'Mother Church'. I would ask him to meditate on Chapter 66: 13 of Isaiah where God says: 'As a mother comforts her child, so I shall comfort you'; and to meditate also on Luke 13: 34, where Jesus speaks of himself in relation to us humans as a hen to her chicks: 'Jerusalem, Jerusalem, you that kill the prophets and stone those who are sent to you! How often have I longed to gather your children together, as a hen gathers her brood under her wings, and you refused!' I beseech Cardinal Connell, having listened to the clucking and felt the warmth of the nest, to allow the maternal feminine in his own placid nature to come to the fore and so assuage the harsh tones of his many rebukes to those of us who are *different*. We *Different Irish* – can you hear me? – we need our new Cardinal to be not only a mother with her chicks but also a mother who even at this late, arctic hour before midnight in the life of humanity might choose to comfort his brood with the wild dignity of affection.

February 7, 2001

TRAVELLERS

In a recent interview in *The Irish Times* with Vincent Browne, Martin Collins, the well-known spokesman for Travellers, who himself works in Pavee Point Travellers Centre, described the significance of what he called 'the Journey'. Martin said to Vincent: 'for many travellers it is the journey that matters, being on the road with their families and extended families. It's growth and development and camaraderie; it's all that stuff that happens on the journey.'

To which Vincent, in Vincent's unique West Limerick mode of groaning, asked: 'What's so enjoyable about the journey?'

If I had been Martin Collins I'd have groaned back: 'But Vincent I've just told you! Why are you asking the question to the answer when I have already just now given you the answer ... *being on the road with their families and extended families. It's growth and development and camaraderie; it's all that stuff that happens on the journey.*'

But Martin Collins, being a more patient man than I,

repeated himself for Vincent's benefit. He said 'Travellers attach a lot of importance to the journey. Also there is the fact that if Travellers feel tied to one location it puts pressure on them.'

I feel an affinity with Martin Collins's concept of 'the Journey' and yet I am a member of what is called 'the Settled Community'. That is to say, I lodge in a house that does not move and I eat cornflakes and I wear pyjamas.

But is there really such a thing as 'the Settled Community'? Are we human beings not all of us longing to be making 'the Journey' as defined by Martin Collins? Are we not all of us Travellers, in our deepest, buried, innermost human feelings?

When we are children and adolescents, every day and every hour of every day is a journey. I am seven years of age and the staircase is a journey in which I can spend all day travelling up and down the stairs, up and down the banisters. Travelling from one room to another is another journey. It's a long way from the kitchen to the bedroom and there is much that can happen along the way; life-altering happenings like sitting down half-way up the stairs at the ninth brass stair-rod. When I am nine I build a tigeen in the back garden. Then I build a tigeen in the living room. Anything for a tigeen. Sometimes my father drives up into the Dublin hills and stops in a forest and my mother produces a picnic and we do this because of the seeds of Traveller spirit within our souls.

In the summertime our parents rent a houseen in Enniscrone in Co. Sligo where I'll meet – I am told – my first Protestants from the North. The Presbyterian Minister, Rev. Rowan and his family from Omagh, Co. Tyrone. What a journey that will prove to be!

And now I am twelve and I want to erect a tent in the sandhills of Enniscrone with my friend Mattie Moran whose sister Fionnuala I'm mad about and we sleep a whole night long in the tent (but no sign of Fionnuala) and I wake early in the morning and stepping out of the tent at dawn I feel that consanguinity with all of Nature and Time – Traveller's Bliss: Immortal Freedom. The second night it rains a downpour and, in the morning, out of the black clouds appears my father roaring like Abraham and he beats the daylights out of me and maybe the reason is that he himself is doing his best to be a member of the Settled Community but he is not succeeding because he knows that he in himself is a Traveller and that his own Mayo father was born in a ditch on the side of the road.

In the beginning of time, which was not so very long ago, we humans here in Ireland were all travellers, aboriginals, indians, booley people, Christ-wanderers. That is to say: we spent part of the year on the move and part of the year in one place. But in time, we became lazy and we repressed the wandering parts of our souls and we erased certain fundamental human values and we placed greater and greater importance on 'settling' until we have now reached the stage where we call ourselves 'the Settled Community'.

But actually we – the Settled Community – are very *unsettled*. Truth to tell, we are 'the Unsettled Community'. The more settled we become, the more unsettled we become and our children, desperate to make their own journeys, take to rugby and kicking one another to death or to drugs or to drink or to overdosing on the Internet or to money, money, money or to 'uniting Germany' or 'uniting Ireland' or some such hocus-pocus.

The so-called Traveller Problem in Ireland is as much a Settled Community problem. It's we couch potatoes, we stick-in-the-muds, we armchair generals, we security freaks who have the problem; we need urgently to find our Traveller roots – to go back to our original Traveller feelings and let go of our property mania and all the connected and related manias. Yes, most of us including myself will go on living mostly urban lives but we will have retrieved our Traveller roots and so we will break our addiction to property and television and we will cease to fear and attack the Permanent Travellers.

We – the Settled Community – having begged the Good God for humility, we should go baseball caps in hands to Pavee Point and ask Martin Collins and his fellow Travellers to give us night classes in 'Finding Our Traveller Roots'. Pavee Point should offer us settled folk 'Rehabilitation Courses'.

I am lucky in that many years ago I discovered that on one side of my family we were actually Tinkers up until quite recently. I say 'Tinkers' for that was the old term for Traveller and it was a dignified term, not a term of abuse. The Tinkers were people who lived in horse-drawn caravans and whose men folk were masters in the ancient arts of tin-smithing: of fixing, mending, making anything to do with tin.

Around the same time I also discovered that on another side of my family we were Protestants. I could hardly believe my luck. A Protestant Tinker! And so it was that when I came to write my book called *Christmas Day* I was able to describe myself as 'a Protestant Tinker'.

Alas other writers, all of them 'Settled Writers' – 'Settled Novelists' and 'Settled Poets' – thought I was joking.

I often find that to be the case with the Settled Community when you try to tell them something very simple and straightforward like 'I am A Protestant Tinker'. Likewise when the Traveller spokesman tried to tell a member of the Settled Community – namely, Vincent Browne – the simple meaning of the phrase 'the Journey' Vincent Browne appeared unable to comprehend and so Martin Collins had to repeat the answer: 'It's growth and development and camaraderie; it's all that stuff that happens on the journey.'

February 21, 2001

LAST DAY IN NEW YORK CITY

Last Saturday week I woke up in a ground-floor bedroom in Manhattan on West Ninetieth Street between Amsterdam Avenue and Columbus Avenue to realise with apprehension that it was to be my last day in New York. Apprehension because of the butterflies that go with all travel but also because of the grief of leaving New York after having had such a brilliant time there with my extravagantly generous host, Colm Tóibín, and, likewise, down in Washington with the mighty Gallivan sisters, Monica and Mary from Newbridge, Co. Kildare. I'd gone over to give a poetry recital in Columbia, Maryland, at the invitation of Catherine McLoughlin-Hayes, Chairperson of HoCoPo LitSo.

I'll say that again, I'll say that again with relish, slowly: Ho-Co-Po-Lit-So. Howard County Poetry and Literature Society. Catherine from Strokestown, Co. Roscommon has been organising events in Maryland for twenty-three years and, with that heart of hers as big as Croke Park, no more hardworking, efficient, hospitable organiser could you meet.

She brought in an audience of six to seven hundred people on a Friday night. A Strokestown lady the soft clay of whose voice is so feathery Roscommon it's as if she'd never flown the nest thirty years ago.

My last day in New York. Oh no! I drag myself out of bed, shower, dress. I slip out to the diner on the corner of West Ninetieth Street and Columbus Avenue.

The Columbus Star Bagel Deli. The Italian guy behind the counter catches my order: 'French toast and grapefruit juice and no coffee.'

'No coffee? It's free and you don't want it? Stay or go?'

'Stay,' I snap back.

French toast is toast soaked in egg and lathered in Maple Syrup. Gustingly tasty.

I head out into the freezing day. Pure blue skies and sunlight but with a cheekbone-chewing wind. I head eastward along West Ninetieth Street until I arrive at Central Park West, cross the street and climb uphill through the bare trees of Central Park up onto the running track that circles the reservoir.

In all of New York this is my hallowed place: the reservoir in Central Park. Today it is two-thirds frozen over and the geese and ducks are all snuggled up, heads in their wings, on the causeway that cuts across the reservoir from southeast to northwest.

I catch hold of the wire netting that surrounds the reservoir and I hang out of it, praising God and giving thanks for this day that is in it. Obeying the notice, I walk around the reservoir 'counter-clockwise'. The joggers pad past me, some of them sprinting, some crawling. On the far side walking parallel to Fifth Avenue, I gaze back across the water to the West Side and the twin towers of the El Dorado apartment block with its white pinnacles. So this is where Stalin's architects got their inspiration from for the Ukraine Hotel and Moscow State University and the Foreign Ministry skyscraper. I give praise also to all the cherry trees along the east shore, presented to the city by one Otto Marx. (No relation, comrade.) Soon these glowing boughs will be snowing blossom and I think of Colm Tóibín in West Ninetieth Street and enviously I contemplate the pleasures ahead of him in New York in the springtime.

He has advised me I should get a cab at 3.30 p.m. to take me to the JFK Airport shuttle bus at Port Authority on Eighth Avenue and Forty-second Street.

At 2.30 p.m. I scamper out again to the diner and ask for a tall latté to take away. Back in the ground-floor front room I spend the last hour sipping the hot milky coffee and watching passers-by watching me (Colm Tóibín is not a man for such fig-leaves as curtains) and listening to, as much as watching, the white walls of the apartment and the reproduction of the Francis Bacon painting of the *Double Portrait of Lucien Freud and Frank Auerbach*. I rejoice in how Francis Bacon catches the beauty as well as the terror of megalatropolitan life.

On the corner of West Ninetieth and Columbus I stand with my overweight suitcase and my forty carrier bags. Within less than a minute a Yellow Cab pulls in.

The driver is about the same age as myself, just a little younger, tall, lean, black as his leather jacket with a blue sheen from his skin that matches his blue jeans.

'Where you from?' he croons.

'Ireland.'

'Island?'

'No, Ireland.'

'Where is Island?'

'It's in the sea near England.'

'Of course it's in the sea, man. Island isn't it?'

'No, IRE-Land.'

'I don't know it, I just don't know it, man.'

Silence while I wrestle with my humiliation. With zest

and humour the driver has put me in my place or, rather, not in my place. Here I am, returning today to the Land of Adams and Trimble and Ahern and Quinn and Harney and where Fine Gael has purged the ablest leader it ever had, John Bruton, and the Archbishop of Dublin has been made a Cardinal, and the driver has never heard of this Land. He's not the only one. Last May in San Francisco in Chinatown I bought two pairs of slippers from a bright, smiling Chinese lady who with quilted delicacy informed me that she was certain she neither knew nor had ever heard of a country called Ireland.

In the back of the taxi I lean forward and, trying to pick up the broken vase of my identity – yippee! – I ask the driver where he is from himself.

'Haiti' – he shouts with delight. 'My father is white just like you are, man, but my mother is black, just like me.'

And he rubs his face, caressing it. He continues crooning.

'God bless America! I live in Brooklyn but I drive Yellow Cab weekends in Manhattan to put four hundred dollars in my pocket. Five days a week I sell real estate. On Sundays I says to my daughter – she's at law school – and my son – he's at High School – I says to them: Well, you tell me now what you've been reading all this week. And they tell me because they know they gotta tell me. And I says to them: You not gonna live in Brooklyn, you gonna live in Manhattan. And they tell me what they been reading all week at school. And they know they not go partying on weeknights. They go partying only on Saturday and I drive them there and I pick 'em up. I'm not a mean man. I tell them, man – school is a *humanitarian* place where you learn how to live as well as to learn. *Humanitarian*, man. Know what I mean? So, they won't be living in Brooklyn, they'll be living in Manhattan. God bless America!'

Before I left Ireland I'd booked an aisle seat on the return flight. Adventurous Irishman! The woman in the inside seat is about forty and thin and dark and handsome and pleasantly she introduces herself and she tells me she's a New Yorker and she voted for George W. Bush because in her own words 'Clinton did nothing for the country'. She adds that she has no interest in Clinton's personal life and thinks it's nobody's business. She doesn't watch television or read newspapers except the local broadsheet.

Today's headlines proclaim that Bush has bombed Iraq. *Don't Mess With Dubya* screams the *New York Post* – and I hear myself besieging her with my account of the current problems of the world and about the Middle East and Africa and Aids. I pontificate: 'Aids is destroying Africa.'

She murmurs: 'I've had it for twenty years.'

'You've –?'

'I've had Aids for twenty years.'

I stop. I stammer. I close my eyes. I shake my head. As gently as possible I congratulate her on her courage and on how well she is looking. Silence. Silence. And then we continue chatting at breakneck speed about our two lives for two and a half hours until she falls asleep.

Today is Ash Wednesday: *O Lord, on my forehead, teach me in these coming forty days to be less of an idiot, even if only by a few millimetres. Teach me to see life in perspective and in proportion. Help me to reduce my hypocrisy levels by even a few millimetres. Teach me to practise as well as to say the Serenity Prayer: Grant me the serenity to accept the things I cannot change, the courage to change the things I can, and the wisdom to know the difference. Marvellous Haiti New York Yellow Cab Driver, dearest beautiful New York Lady with Aids, more than either of you I am dust and unto dust I shalt return. Pray for me.*
February 28, 2001

THE HEATHER BLAZING

Saturday, February 24, five days before Foot-and-Mouth is confirmed in South Armagh: Room 210 in White's Hotel in Wexford town, my alarm ringing for 8.30 a.m.

It is the morning after the poetry recital at the Welsh Academy the night before and my muscles are purring with tidal waters of relief. I got through it! Again! Every poetry recital is a Beecher's Brook and in the days leading up to it there are nightmare glimpses of that Himalayan crevasse as it comes galloping out to devour you. No matter how many times you may have jumped it before, each time is always the first time and you try not to think about it and, when you've jumped it, you wonder how you did it and the sense of relief purifies.

Blue skies and a gold sun as I hit the road for Dublin. As I squeeze my foot on the accelerator coming down onto the bridge at Ferrycarraig, I reckon I should be back in Dublin by lunchtime. Oh you stupid man! What's so smart about being back in Dublin by lunchtime? What's the hurry? Don't you realise how fortunate you are to be down here in County

Wexford? Take off your blinkers. Take your foot off the accelerator and slow down. Take it easy, man.

Easier said than done, 'Take it easy, man.' Ease, easy, easiness: oddballs on the highway.

Slowing down to a steady 40 m.p.h. I notice the first stirrings of the gorse and all the trees and hedges rufous with pregnancy. Inching into the town of Enniscorthy I behold the mental hospital on top of the hill on the right. What a prima donna pile! All that pain going on inside those walls and, yet, you might think it was the Pope's Irish holiday residence; it's tall graceful Italian bell-towers of red and white brick and it's elegant rooftops. What was the thinking of the lunatic asylum architects? Castel Gandolfo, Enniscorthy.

Enniscorthy, itself an Italian hilltop town, announces 'Disc Parking'. I crawl up and down the town searching for a non-disc-parking car-park. Near the top of the town I drive into a car-park on rough ground. I ask a lady if I need a disc. 'Oh you do,' she laughs, 'but you can have mine and there's nearly an hour left on it.' She runs off uphill and I jump out after her. Full of laughter, she hands it to me. I stand there in shock, a Dublin lunatic unused to such courtesy and mirth.

Entering the town at the bottom of the hill I spotted a SuperValu. I'll shop first and then I'll walk the town. The SuperValu is spick and span, spacious, well stocked, well staffed. A far cry from my local Sandymount Tesco where you have to climb around boxes and pallets in order to find anything and where you can always be sure that some of the staples you're looking for will not be on the shelves and where it is so understaffed that the surviving staff always look as if they are under siege as well as underpaid. As I march merrily out of the Enniscorthy SuperValu, little do I know that tomorrow afternoon in Tesco in Phibsborough I will stand in a line of twenty-seven customers because there is nobody on the Express checkout.

The streets of Enniscorthy would lift anybody's heart. At

the bottom of the hill the castle overlooking the River Slaney and, next to it, the beautiful Athenaeum and on to the Market Square with its mighty Father Murphy monument and, to the right, Murphy Flood's hotel. Imagine having a name like Murphy Flood. Paul Murphy Flood. Now there's a name that might have got me somewhere. Paul Durcan, how are ye! Away with the Durcans and on with the Murphy Floods! At the head of the Market Square the offices of the County Council and the UDC. Many's the big election meeting must have been held here. De Valera or Seán Lemass at the microphone and Mícheál Tóibín in the Chair.

I head up Main Street to St Aidan's Cathedral whose spire is awe-inspiring. The awe-inspiring spire of the Cathedral of the Diocese of Ferns. As I reach the first palings, my knees gasping, I grab hold of them and behold a fountain in the churchyard. A fountain in an Irish churchyard! And not just some anaemic little sprinkler but a virile, sturdy gusher, banging out the suds in one hundred per cent foam and crush. In the gate and around to the fountain and a plaque which reads: 'To The Memory Of Family And Friends Laid To Rest Elsewhere.'

Oh. Such casual, unasked-for, unexpected sweetness makes my day. And I think of Jonathan Philbin Bowman who went home to God just a year ago and that beautiful concept of his: 'daymaker'. Jonathan – Jonathan said – Jonathan wanted to be a 'daymaker': to make your day and my day. And he did, oh he did, God rest his plucky soul. Like Donal McCann, Jonathan Philbin Bowman had an eerily deep understanding of the true meaning of the Crucifixion.

Inside, down the long slender nave at the crossing of the transepts, I find myself in the Alhambra of Enniscorthy. Great, high, painted walls of reds and yellows, blues and greens, all in geometric Arabic stencils, and blue ceilings with stars. And scrolls of episcopal names concluding with *Brendanus* Comiskey. And a Tricolour in a holster, just like a

Union Jack in a Church of Ireland. And on the altar a vast, handmade orange carpet. In the Lady Chapel I light five candles for my dead friends: John Meagher, Patrick Nugent, Michael Hartnett, Francis Stuart, Donal McCann.

I try to pray but staring at the statue of Our Lady I am unable. I hear Donal growling at me: 'What's the matter with you? Haven't you just met her outside in the car-park when full of laughter she gave you her parking disc!' Our Lady of Parking Discs, have mercy on me.

Back outside the cathedral, I gaze up at the Duffry Gate. I walk along the terrace of Duffry Hill and four ten-year-old boys come hurtling towards me on rollerblades. Steep streets to be rollerblading in! Two girls come strolling behind the boys and the one licking a lollipop smiles at me and explains 'they're crazy'.

On Rafter Street I step into The Baked Potato and I get a proper toasted ham sandwich and a hot cup of real coffee in a warm atmosphere; a rare combination in these chilly, pre-packaged times.

Back to the car and over the river and up Vinegar Hill. At the top, all around the illegible 1798 Memorial, not a bin in sight and oodles of litter. Carrier bags of beer cans and vodka bottles. But, all around, the horizons are drawn in crayon and pencil. To the west the Blackstairs Mountains and the Duffry in the Barony of Scarawalsh; the *Tír Dubh*, the Black Country, the villages of Rathnure and Killann where my boyhood heroes, the hurlers Nick and Bobbie and Willie Rackard, hailed from. This be countryside to equal Provence and it has found its Cézanne in the writings of Colm Tóibín – whose mountain-scape, though, is the sea to the east at Ballyconnigar, Curracloe, Cush, Blackwater – author of *The Blackwater Lightship* shortlisted on Monday for the £100,000 IMPAC prize.

I drive on towards Gorey thinking how I will turn left and west at Gorey and go out the seven miles into the hills and visit Donal McCann in his grave in Monaseed and say hallo to his beloved relations Geraldine and Jimmy Berney. Simultaneously I begin to think of good reasons for driving straight on for Dublin. I was with Welsh people in White's Hotel last night, February 23. It is four days before the discovery of Foot-and-Mouth in South Armagh but even so I might constitute a threat to the Berney farm. Again I hear Donal growling: 'So you're afraid of transmitting Foot-and-Mouth to a dead man, are you?' All that can save me now is Donal himself in the guise of my guardian angel and he does just that. On the edge of Gorey I hit the tail of a traffic jam and so I take the left turn without having to think, and away I curl along the banks of the River Bann up into the hills of Monaseed.

At the grave of Donal McCann: bird-song, sheep-bleat, silence. I ask Donal for his forgiveness for hurt I caused him in his terrestrial life and for his help in fighting my own demons and I thank him for all the good times we had. I meet a lady at the gate, Mrs Wadding, the sacristan I think, and she kindly promises to tell the Berney family how I could not call on account of the Foot-and-Mouth.

And I drive on through Monaseed past the National School, founded in 1913 and flying high the European flag on its own. Past the Myles Byrne Memorial Hall; Myles, who was born in Monaseed, fought for Napoleon and is buried in Montmartre. I turn right for Coolgreaney and Arklow and motor as slowly as I can – 30 m.p.h. – along the ridge up and down the lane for miles and miles savouring the valley below; and the mountains beyond, Annagh Hill and Croghan Mountain are greeting me. Just like yesterday afternoon, driving the lanes of Wexford town, I shouted to a woman 'Where's White's Hotel?' And she cried back 'Down there,' and she smiled at the baffled patch of my face and she added 'We met you on the plane from Vancouver – welcome to Wexford!' Yes, yes, yes – the Wexford couple who'd picked out Vancouver Island on the Internet and spent three weeks driving up and down that Pacific wilderness and had the times of their lives. How I'd admired them for their imagination, their independence, their audacity. The heather blazing!

> *At Boolevogue as the sun was setting*
> *O'er the bright May meadows of Shelmalier,*
> *A rebel hand set the heather blazing*
> *And brought the neighbours from far and near.*
>
> *March 7, 2001*

BALTHUS

We were married in 1969 but it was to be ten years before we could afford to go on our honeymoon. At the time we did not feel we were missing out catastrophically, but maybe ten years is a bit long to wait for your honeymoon, even for a pair of stoical young lovers like ourselves. Five years further on down the long road, our marriage ended and we had to go our separate ways and I ask myself: was it because we had to wait all those ten years for our honeymoon? We lived not on a shoestring but on twenty or thirty shoestrings, and shoestrings tend to wear thin and to snap. The attrition of never having a penny to spare. The know-alls, however, in my family and outside it, knew better; their mile-long noses oblivious to such things as shoestrings, they pronounced that the break-up was due to 'Paul's flawed character'. The vultures of marriage, as of art, always know better; which is to say they always know nothing.

Our honeymoon was a week in Paris in June 1979. Rosslare-Fishguard-London-Dover-Calais-Paris. Wednesday,

June 13, 1979; The Gare du Nord! I was thirty-four years old. I had never been in Paris before. As I levitated in the Gare du Nord, I felt an enchantment that not even the devoutest Christian or Jew or Muslim could feel on entering the Jaffa Gate into Jerusalem.

For the next seven days that excitement grew until its concentric circles spread out their peripheries so far beyond my soul that only at the hour of my death am I likely to glean their extent.

We had reserved a room in a *pension* on the Right Bank, off the Rue de Rivoli in a little street called the Rue St Bon. There was nothing that was not good about everything on that street: the smells of hot bread tinged with odours of red wine and roast coffee. At one end of the street stood the Tour St Jacques where in the Middle Ages pilgrims used assemble for the year-long pilgrimage to Santiago de Compostela. At the other end of the street was a flight of steps opening out onto the newly built national arts centre, the Pompidou Centre or 'the Beaubourg' as it was known.

The Beaubourg, 1979! What a revolution in my soul! For seven days we lived in the Beaubourg, riding the famous glass escalators, drinking and eating Modern Art and sitting in the Plaza watching the mime artists. The Paris-Moscow 1900–1933 Exhibition was also on in the Beaubourg and here I saw for the first time the pictures of Martiros Saryan the Armenian genius, the early paintings of Chagall and *The Dance* by Matisse loaned from Leningrad. I took my laughing wife in my arms and flew with her over the Eiffel Tower. The following year we returned with our two daughters aged eleven and ten and the following year and the following year; all thanks to Madame Kathleen Bernard who loaned us her apartment in the sixteenth *arrondissement* and the Belgian priest Father Jean Greisch who loaned us his apartment in the thirteenth.

It was in the Beaubourg that I discovered Modern

European Art: Matisse, Picasso, Malevich, Soutine, Derain, Dubuffet, Miró, Giacometti and, first and last and above all, Balthus.

Who? I had never heard of nor read a word in Ireland about Balthus, and I was to find over the next twenty years that while a few knew the name Balthus few knew his paintings, although his paintings were to be seen in the great galleries of the world. Balthus. B-A-L-T-H-U-S. I played with the name as a child plays with its teddy bear.

In June 1979 there were two paintings by Balthus in the Beaubourg. *Cathy Dressing*, painted in 1933 when Balthus was twenty-five – based on a scene from *Wuthering Heights* by Emily Brontë, with Heathcliff, Cathy and the maid Nelly. Balthus's painting is a depiction of what was to become one of the basic stories in all his work: the relationship between Man and Woman and their apparently irreconcilable differences. I say 'apparently' because the cadence of his painting technique means that no clinically rational or smart-alec conclusion can be arrived at. With classical clarity, Balthus depicts the mystery of the relationship.

The second Balthus painting was called *The Turkish Room*, painted in 1966 when the painter was fifty-eight. It depicts a room in detail, incorporating a portrait of a naked, young Japanese woman in an open, pink dressing gown reclining on a bed. I say 'incorporating' because one of the glories of this painting, and of all of the works of Balthus, is that she is but part of the larger picture, just as you or I at any given moment in time are but part of the larger picture.

The Japanese woman is seen in profile against a wall of glazed blue tiles with geometric designs of blue petals, green petals, white lozenges, black lozenges, gold bars. A quarter of the wall is taken up by a brown two-arched window with green, louvred shutters – shutters with those wooden slats you see all over France and Italy. The floor also is glazed tile of a grand geometric pattern: red triangles, black triangles, white triangles.

The Japanese woman is holding out at arms length a Japanese mirror of polished metal, and later over the years you may learn or not learn that the mirror is a symbol of the woman's soul. At the foot of the bed a stand holds a white dish of six eggs. Nearby stands a green wrought-iron table with a tall, lean vase and a small, white eggcup.

On our honeymoon in June 1979 we spent hours staring at these canvasses and over the intervening twenty years I have returned to them again and again, as I have also to the 1982 painting called *The Painter and His Model*, which is a mystical vision of the reality of art in all our lives. An elderly man with his back to us is opening the curtains. In the foreground, a Rubik's Cube on a table and a girl kneeling on the floor at a chair, browsing. My daughter Sarah, now herself a painter, used then at the age of thirteen kneel on the gallery floor copying Balthus. Then, as now, she admired Balthus as much as I did.

If there is solid ground in my own poetry I owe it partly to the thousands of hours I have spent before the paintings of Balthus and browsing his catalogues. Just as he, Balthus, by his own admission, owed much of all he learned from thousands of hours spent staring at the frescoes of Piero della Francesca in Arezzo in Tuscany. Only last month in New York I made my fourth pilgrimage to see *The Mountain*, which Balthus painted in 1937 aged twenty-nine and which is his greatest hymn to the Man-Woman mystery. It hangs in the Metropolitan Museum in Central Park but I had first encountered it at the Realism exhibition in the Beaubourg in 1981. For twenty years I have been looking at and thinking about *The Mountain* by Balthus and thank God I cannot explain it. It is like a Brian Friel play; a Brian Friel dream play. On the grassy mountaintop stands an exultant Catherine Byrne in a long grey dress and her hands joined above her head of golden hair. To her left kneels a man with a rucksack who could be a husband who has waited ten years for his honeymoon. To her right and behind her, a younger man gazing up at her. Behind him on the edge of a precipice, an elderly married couple enthusiastically peering down into the abyss. At Catherine Byrne's feet, a young woman asleep. And far off, almost out-of-sight, top right, a man walking away; he might be yet another ten-years-waiting-for-his-honeymoon husband.

Balthus died three weeks ago on Sunday, February 18.

He was the greatest western painter of the twentieth century, alongside his friend and admirer Picasso who in 1937 bought for his own private collection a painting by Balthus called *Les Enfants* – The Children. Yet another painstakingly painted depiction of the male-female relationship; this time a boy and a girl, the girl kneeling on the floor reading a book, the boy kneeling on a chair at a table gazing into infinity. Is Balthus telling us a story in which the cards are already stacked in favour of the girl? Either way, what he is doing is depicting the galactic boredom of adolescence, the eternities of daydreaming, the day-to-day mystery of innocence and experience which makes terrified, insouciant children of us all. Before he died Picasso made a gift to the Louvre of *Les Enfants* by Balthus to whom he once remarked 'You have the secret of creating an intimate atmosphere – I don't.' On a separate occasion Picasso remarked 'Nobody can paint a portrait the way Balthus can.'

Balthus, born February 29, 1908, Paris, died February 18, 2001, Switzerland. His son Stanislas, in 1983, composed his father's epitaph: 'Balthus aspires to the anonymous perfection of the man liberated from the burden of himself.' God be praised for the great works of art which Balthus created out of nothing. Peace to his soul.

March 14, 2001

THE AUTOBIOGRAPHY OF JOHN MORIARTY

On Thursday January 31, 1985 Radio 1 transmitted one of the most historic interviews ever broadcast by RTÉ. That evening in his series *Dialogue* Andy O'Mahony introduced the interview with these words: 'My guest tonight is one of the most remarkable people that I've ever met in my entire life.' That is not the sort of language one associates with Andy O'Mahony, most sceptical, sober, professional of broadcasters and the last broadcaster on earth who would indulge in hyperbole or sound-byte. His guest was John Moriarty whom Andy O'Mahony went on to describe as 'a philosopher by training and a mystic by vocation, he earns his living as a gardener ...'

Almost exactly sixteen years later, today, this very day, Wednesday March 21, is the publication day of *Nostos*, the first volume of the autobiography of John Moriarty, published in a beautiful hardback edition by The Lilliput Press at the economical price of £25. I say 'economical' because this is a mighty book in every sense of that mighty word 'mighty'. This book is almost seven hundred pages but that is as straw compared with the scale of its contents: its stories, its poems, its memories, its prayers, its laughter, its tears, its songs, its passions, its citations, its *dindsenchas*, its thought, its insight, its fun, its madness, its celebrations, its meditations, its terrible suffering, its amazing physical presence, its amazing spirituality. Just as Andy O'Mahony was indulging in no idle exaggeration on that January night sixteen years ago, I am indulging in no idle hyperbole when I say that this autobiography by John Moriarty is one of the most remarkable autobiographies I have ever read in my life.

And yet you can search reference books and not find the name John Moriarty: reputable reference books by cultural historians and journalists. Why is this? Because John Moriarty is that almost extinct species in the Western World – the man who thinks for himself; the man who feels, imagines, journeys and responds through instinct and affection. In Patrick Kavanagh's words:

> *He knew that posterity has no use*
> *For anything but the soul,*
> *The lines that speak the passionate heart,*
> *The spirit that lives alone.*

So then who is this lover of women and faithful friend, of whom his dear mother used say to her neighbour Greta: 'What with his drainpipe trousers and long hair, he doesn't even look like a fact of life'? Who every year of his life wherever he was in the world, and often as not penniless, would take ship and bus and, at the borders of North Kerry, walk the last miles home to be with his parents and their eleven cows for Christmas time? Who is this man who sings his way on a bike through life; who lonesome in Manitoba recalls being in court in Listowel for not having a light on his bike and how he had pleaded 'Please, your honour, there was in the song I was singing enough light for me and for anyone coming against me'? Who is this man who late one night in a pool hall in Flagstaff, Arizona, standing in the background, sees the local tough guy walk across the room to him and say: 'I guess you're in my way'? Who is this man who lives not only his own life but also the lives of Darwin, Nietzsche, Melville and Dylan Thomas, hoping at all times to redeem those great souls from their dreadful fates? Who is this king of nature writers who can write of dragonflies: 'Like cart axles, their heads held their eyes in place'?

Who is John Moriarty? I would like you to imagine if A. J. F. O'Reilly – Tony O'Reilly (let the sniggerers out there snigger but I am in earnest, for O'Reilly and Moriarty were the two outstanding students of their generation in University College Dublin) – imagine if after graduating from UCD Tony O'Reilly had never gone into business and instead disappeared off the face of the known world only to surface thirty years later as a poet-philosopher-mystic-storyteller who had spent all those years walking the roads of the world in search not only of his own soul but of the soul of the world.

O'Reilly was comparable to Moriarty not only in brilliant intelligence, wit, presence but also in his extraordinary appearance. That is to say, both men were extraordinarily handsome: the one the tall, curly, redheaded athlete from the north suburbs of Dublin with the look of a young Greek god; the other a tall, dark, longhaired gentle giant from a small farm in North Kerry, also with the look of a young Greek god.

Last week I spoke with one of Ireland's leading economists, Professor Dermot McAleese, himself a man of rare good sense, and when I asked him for his own memory of John Moriarty in UCD he answered slowly, proudly with two words: '*Gentle* and *deep*.' I spoke also with the design consultant Helen O'Neill and she too recalled a man 'who never saw badness in you, who had complete trust in you, who was magical'. She recalled his way of greeting you: 'He'd smile and he'd raise his hand and he'd cry "Christ, I bring the thunder."'

The purpose of the analogy with Tony O'Reilly is to demonstrate the *stature* of John Moriarty. But there is an irony too. A recurring motif of Moriarty's autobiography is that Western man's most dangerous mistake has been to see all of life as an economic opportunity. It is not that Moriarty proposes some absurd Peter Pan fantasy whereby man does not live and grow by bread, work, adventure, exploration. No, it is that Moriarty has long seen a vision of the reality of the Western World in which our very metabolism has been poisoned by seeing life itself as an economic opportunity. Moriarty believes that 'modern culture has left us helpless before the contents of our own minds'. He refuses to be, as he says, 'conscripted' into the modern Western World; he refuses, as he puts it, 'psychic topiary'. Refusing to be 'a potted plant', he has spent his sixty-three years seeking his 'bush soul'.

John Moriarty was born in Moyvane in North Kerry in 1938, on a small farm of eleven cows, the fourth of six children to James Moriarty and Mary O'Brien. His early and by far his most important education was at St Michael's in Listowel, to and from which he cycled seven and three-quarter miles every day and where he learned to read Greek and Latin as well as Irish and English. In UCD he enrolled in philosophy. He rarely attended lectures and spent most of his time in the National Library, absorbing the great books of the world; in the solitude of his room in Rathmines; sitting in the Main Hall of Earlsfort Terrace talking and, as his friend Michael Hartnett put it, 'pursuing his amatory affairs'.

After taking a double first-class honours degree, he went to London where, living from hand to mouth, he walked the streets by night and slept in a library near Leicester Square by day. A chance encounter with the renowned English philosopher J. D. Cameron brought an invitation from Cameron to join the Philosophy Department at Leeds University from which two years later he was head-hunted by the Department of English in the University of Manitoba in Winnipeg. After six years in Winnipeg he decided that the academic life was the wrong life for him and he took to the road of the pilgrim poet-philosopher, living from the age of thirty-three to this day from hand to mouth. That initial sleeping-rough episode in London in 1963 was the first of a chain of such episodes in England, Canada, the USA, Mexico, Greece, Rome, Connemara, Kerry, Oxford and Kildare. In 1994 The Lilliput Press published the first of his great works of philosophical storytelling, *Dreamtime*. This has been followed by three more works: *Turtle was Gone a Long Time*, volumes one, two and three.

But it is with today's publication of his autobiography that John Moriarty comes for the first time fully into the arena and, while I would urge you to read this book most of all for its own sake and its own sake alone, I would commend to you the autobiography as an introduction to his other books. For it is here in this un-put-downable autobiography that we see John Moriarty working out his thrilling spirituality in the context of his ordinary day-to-day living.

I say 'thrilling spirituality'. The autobiography resembles *Anam Cara* by John O'Donohue. Indeed *Anam Cara* could be described as a Rough Guide to John Moriarty and, at one time, O'Donohue was a disciple of Moriarty or, to put it in more ordinary words, Moriarty was a 'mentor' of John O'Donohue. 'Mentor' of course is a great football word and an admirer of both O'Donohue and Moriarty once remarked to me that whereas O'Donohue is First Division football, Moriarty is Premier League.

The only other books remotely comparable to John Moriarty's autobiography are Thomas Merton's *Seven Storey Mountain* (published in London under the title *Elected*

Silence), the same author's *Asian Journal* and *Woodbrook* by David Thomson. The two books by Merton describe the spiritual journeys of that heroic Cistercian monk. Thomson's *Woodbrook* is the story of the young English tutor in the big house Woodbrook in Co. Roscommon and his romance with his pupil Phoebe Kirkwood.

There are such courtship stories in Moriarty's autobiography. He explains why it is that he feels morally unable ever to marry although it is what he longs for. The *nostos* (meaning 'homecoming') of the title is his final recognition of his beloved parents as the parents he chose. In the last pages Moriarty discovers that his own story is in fact a voyage to his father and mother, bringing him home to them not only in their dying but also in the act of writing this book. In prose worthy of Rembrandt, Moriarty depicts his father's requiem for his wife. The reader is the privileged witness of, in Eliot's words 'the purification of the motive/In the ground of our beseeching'.

Moriarty has paid a terrible price for his spiritual courage. He describes without self-pity a nervous breakdown or 'dark night of the soul', at one point in which, on the rack of his bed in a damp cottage in Connemara, when 'I was often too weak to pray, and I'd open the Bible flat out on a chair and I'd ask it to pray for me'.

The fundamental question of his story is: has Western Man 'come to an evolutionary dead end'? Moriarty's answer is optimistic, provided we each have it in us to undergo Gethsemane. Moriarty is emphatically *not* 'a born-again Christian'. He is a man who after a lifetime's sometimes wonderful, sometimes hilarious, sometimes tragic struggle has become a Christian for the first time. He sees Christ as the Hero of Evolution and he hears Christ beseeching humanity to follow Christ out of official Christianity into a new evolution of mankind in which man will cease to be hostile to his environment and instead become part of nature again, creaturely as the heron standing midstream at the weir in the river of the Divine.

> *He among them nightly moving*
> *Watched her members grow,*
> *And crouched beside them,*
> *Cried beseeching –*
> *Let her spirit go.*

Every household in Ireland should have a copy of this magical book.

March 21, 2001

SUMMER TIME

Putting the clock forward on Saturday night and waking up on Sunday morning to Summer Time in Ringsend by the banks of the Liffey, I do not know whether to laugh with anger or to cry with joy. 'Oh go on with you Paul,' whispers my lost love with all her geese at her knees. 'Go on with you Paul.'

Every winter is hard but this last winter has been the hardest. The days were shorter, the nights longer and Ireland seemed a crueller place than it did a year ago. We have become so cruel, greedy, vindictive, spiteful, venomous. I think this new Cruel Ireland was born the day they hounded down Bishop Eamonn Casey. There he was, an average sinning mortal like us all, only he was kinder than most, and we hounded him and we spent about three years devouring him and when we were sated with his blood we licked our lips and we went on to the next quarry, Charlie Haughey, and the next and the next. But it all began with Eamonn Casey. I wonder where he is now – the poor man. Will he ever forgive us? Doubtless he will, being the sort that he is, but we do not deserve it. If Rome had a clue about the thirst for Christ-like Christianity in Ireland, wouldn't they have made Eamonn Casey a Cardinal instead of good-man Desmond Connell?

All this winter, only more so than the previous winter, we have had to kowtow to the nasal trumpetings of the Celtic Smarty-pants. And yet in health, education, justice we are going backwards. You would think that well-off people would voluntarily tax themselves in order to contribute to reforms in health and justice but, no, it seems that the wealthier people become, the more selfish they become. And with the purge of John Bruton, Sinn Féin IRA are motoring glamorously into government in Dublin – a mobile phone in one hand and a baseball bat in the other.

As for the Minister of Money himself, Charlie McCreevy, I had the pleasure of spending a night in his company two years ago and he struck me then as a humane, jolly, up-front, decent guy. I cannot for the life of me understand how he can in good conscience preside over such an unjust distribution of wealth. Can it be that he does not really – really – know the reality of life on the chip-shop floor? That our health system is a black circus; that our prison system is a black circus; that our policies on drug addiction and homelessness are a black circus; that our education machine is a black circus; that our towns and cities are ludicrously under-policed; that our litter problem is a black circus; that our non-existent transport system is a *very* black circus. Charlie McCreevy, when you tease us with words like 'pinko', I would ask you to think again and to remember that the gospel message of the Sermon on the Mount is a socialist message and that, therefore, just because the Soviets made a hames of Socialism does not absolve you as Minister of Money from distributing money justly and fairly.

But, Paul, that's all winter stuff! Winter Time is over as of midnight last Saturday. Yes, yes, yes, yes, thank God it's over and may I never see another winter like it again.

But, Paul, have you forgotten the light that saw you through the winter? That astounding gift given you by your daughter Síabhra and her partner Blaise? Away all October, when you came back you found that the filthy, little, black backyard of your cave had been transformed into a beautiful Japanese Zen garden, a small ocean of gravel with a mountain range of rocks in the centre and whitewashed walls and three terracotta pots of montbretia and a jar of thrift and the kitchen door painted Brazilian yellow and a steel mat and a gravel rake. How many winter dawns did you stand at your window feasting on your daughter's gift of light? How many winter twilights did you poultice your soul with a go of the rake in the gravel? So put away that horrible nay-saying dark of another Irish winter and those roof-strangling low grey skies. Light, light, light, light. I jump into my Opel Astra chariot and I leap across South Lotts to Baggot Street Bridge and the most beautiful street in all of Dublin city, perhaps in all of Europe.

Actually it's a street of water: the Grand Canal between Baggot Street Bridge and Leeson Street Bridge. And being the most beautiful walk in Dublin in the springtime, it's as much about sitting down as walking. At the lock-gates at Baggot Street Bridge I lean against the Wilton Terrace arm of the gate and for the millionth time I gaze up at the red-brick house that's actually built on the bridge with the date 1916 in big red-brick numerals. It used be Parson's Bookshop, run by two great ladies Miss O'Flaherty and Miss King, and it was the best bookshop in Dublin in the fifties, the sixties, the seventies, the eighties.

Apart from Ruth Kenny in Books Upstairs on College Green, Miss King was the only bookseller in Dublin who would stock the latest volume on the painter Balthus or the latest radical book on theology or philosophy. I turn around and look up that extraordinary vista to Leeson Street Bridge. I close my eyes and I imbibe the breeze and the sunlight. I open my eyes and I gaze up the aisle of water to the altar of Leeson Street Bridge, an aisle of water which, between arcades of trees, is the nave of a chapel than which there is no nave holier in all of Glendalough and Ferns and Clonmacnoise.

This Baggot Street corner of the canal is the Corner of the Seats. On the Mespil Road side, the seat erected by Friends of Patrick Kavanagh in 1968 with, inscribed in its granite sides, his poem 'Lines Written on a Seat on the Grand Canal, Dublin'. Opposite, on the far side of the Lock, under silver birch, hawthorn and cherry, a seat commemorating Percy French; oddly, this seat occupies the space of the original seat which Kavanagh used sit on and which is the subject of his poem. I often wonder what happened to that seat. Did somebody steal it in the dead of night? Or did it just die? For even a seat must die. About thirty yards upstream from Percy French is the seat with a bronze figure of Kavanagh himself, sitting with arms folded contemplating not just the water in front of him but also the Department of Arts, Heritage, Gaeltacht and the Islands on the Right Bank. When he makes eye contact with Síle de Valera in her office in the treetops, what does Kavanagh say to her: 'I knew your father's father – dacent fella.'

Having walked the eighty yards from Baggot Street Bridge to the lock-gate I sit down on Percy French's seat, cross my legs and pray to Percy. Its inscription reads: 'Songwriter, Artist, Engineer, 1854–1920. *Remember me is all I ask and yet – If the remembrance prove a task, forget.*' I remember you, Percy French; you were a sensational songwriter and poet, a handy landscape artist and – an engineer. You were a good man and a true man of the road, a real troubadour of the Sacred Company of Raftery and Kavanagh.

Paul, this is supposed to be a walk, not a sit-in. Okay. I jump to my feet and stride out, power-walking all the way up to Leeson Street Bridge on whose crown I stand and behold the white gable wall 'Joe Byrne Bets Here – Est. 1917'. One thing in Dublin that has not changed in all of going on one hundred years. Sometimes I read it as 'Lenin Bets Here – Est. 1917' and Joe Byrne lets me have my way. I avert my chaste eyes from the gigantic billboard with its naked woman clutching a bottle of Diet Coke and whispering 'Luck has everything to do with it'. A chaste bow to the Kiosk in the middle of Adelaide Road – another survivor; its awning was the bib of my childhood.

About turn and straight back down to the Corner of the Seats and I sit beside Kavanagh on his seat and think once again of that golden summer in 1967, the summer before he died, and what wonderful company he was – the funniest man, said Brian Lynch – and he was, up there with Buster Keaton and Stan Laurel, and how he encouraged us young poets and how, in my own case, he introduced me to his London publisher.

And I think of that time – only last summer it was – when I brought Jean Kennedy Smith to introduce her to you here. What a Green Fool I made of myself that night. She was staying in the Merrion Hotel and she'd asked me to give her a lift out to Dun Laoghaire and naturally I was delighted since no more down-to-earth and humorous lady could you meet, except possibly on the side of a mountain under a cliff in Achill Island in County Mayo.

When I picked her up at the Merrion Hotel, I said 'Do you mind if I take you on a tiny magical mystery tour?'

'Sure Paul,' she said.

And so at 7.30 p.m. on Saturday evening June 17 last year we drove up to the lock at Baggot Street bridge. Not a sinner around, except Kavanagh himself on his seat. Jean Kennedy Smith was enchanted by the inscription of the poem on the Kavanagh Memorial Seat.

'But' – she exclaimed – 'why aren't there more of them?'

And I, in Einstein mode, said 'More of what?'

'More poems,' she shouted.

As I scoured my silence for words, she added: 'Did you visit my brother Robert's grave in Arlington?'

I winced. 'No, I tried to but I could not find it.'

She said: 'Well, they have a lot of plinths standing around his grave with quotations from his speeches. Why don't you do the same here?' Throwing out her hand over the canal, she said: 'You could have six or seven standing stones of Kavanagh's poems here.'

A vision of Dublin in 4001 AD.

At midnight, about to drive Jean Kennedy Smith back from Dun Laoghaire, I forgot to switch on my driving lights. I could only plead that, in my capacity as chauffeur, I got carried away. She was amused most graciously but she has not asked me for a lift again.

O Patrick, what am I to do? 'Nothing.' What? 'On Paul Durcan my hopes are *pinned*; But wait till he gets his second *wind*.'

March 28, 2001

CHRISTMAS EVE 2001

On the drive out here to the Radio Centre in RTÉ the taxi driver asks: 'Is it Tora Bora you want? Or is it Kabul? Or is it Mesar-e-Sharif?' When I fail to respond, he says: 'Or is it Kandahar?' I stammer a reply: 'No, actually it's Spin Boldak that I'm looking for.' The taxi driver cries: 'Spin Boldak, is it? No better man. Kabul, how are ye! Spin Boldak is your only man!'

Christmas Eve. And tonight, Christmas Morning, 2001, the news headlines will be the same as they have always been for nearly two thousand years: War in the East and a Proclamation in the fourteenth verse of the second chapter of the Gospel according to Saint Luke: 'Glory to God in the highest, and on earth peace to men of good will.' And then on Wednesday we'll have the Stoning of Stephen and on Friday the Massacre of the Innocents.

On Easter Monday 1916 Patrick Pearse, a fanatical, young idealist, set out on what nowadays would be called a suicide terrorist mission. Knowing, indeed praying, that he himself would be executed, and knowing that hundreds if not thousands of innocent civilians would be slaughtered, Pearse led a suicide attack on the city of Dublin to force the British Empire into withdrawing from Ireland. Likewise on September 11, 2001 Muhammad Atta, a fanatical, young Arab idealist, led a suicide attack against the city of New York to force the empire of the USA into withdrawing from the East.

In the eighty-five years between Patrick Pearse and Muhammad Atta, Ireland became the world's number one nursery of terrorism. From Michael Collins to MacStiofain, O'Bradaigh, O'Connell, Twomey, McGuinness and Adams, the IRA became the world's leading and most successful terrorist organisation.

How could anyone, therefore, least of all in Ireland, have been *really* surprised by the hijackings and bombings in New York and Washington and Pennsylvania? In the early 1970s one expected just such acts of war by the PLO and/or the IRA. In those forgotten years the PLO hijacked planes and tortured and murdered and terrified innocent passengers. The IRA went on to develop the theory of what they called 'the spectacular'. They assassinated Lord Mountbatten and his family. They assassinated the British ambassador. They attempted to murder the entire British Government in a Brighton hotel and almost succeeded. They fired rockets into 10 Downing Street. At Enniskillen, Omagh, Warrington, Darkley, Comber, Kingsmills, Claudy, Canary Wharf, et sweet cetera, they massacred and murdered and tortured thousands of innocent people. In 1996, on a blue sunny morning, they blew up the entire city centre of Manchester. These 'spectaculars' are now accepted as but episodes in a Thirty Years War of terror waged by the world's most successful terrorist organization.

Why, then, in the 1970s, 1980s, 1990s did the British Government not form 'a grand coalition' with the USA to wage a war against terror? Why did the British Government and the USA not bomb and 'daisy-cut' Counties Armagh, Tyrone and Derry into oblivion? Into the Oblivion of Afghanistan.

'Och, King Herod, what is the difference between an Irishman and an Afghan man?'

'To tell you the damned jolly truth, I'm damned if I jolly well know! Your average Afghan man is indistinguishable from your average Irishman.'

And so it came to pass in the thirtieth year of the reign of Caesar Augustus that the president of the USA was tangoing with the IRA in the White House, canoodling with the IRA over the very same presidential furniture over which in 1945 President Harry Truman issued that sexy little executive order to incinerate the entire civilian population of Hiroshima and over which George W. Bush ordered the laying waste of Afghanistan. On December 12 the London *Daily Telegraph* reported that 'the sheet metal on the side of one exploded bomb had been inscribed by an American soldier named Gary. It read: "This bomb is gonna shine like a bright light in the goat's ass."'

Eeny meeny miny mo.

I can hear – can you hear? – the laughter of the American pilots of lil' ol' *Enola Gay* over Hiroshima after they'd performed their little obscenity on August 6, 1945.

Why does not a decent plain Irishman like Bertie Ahern try reading the Gospel of Saint Luke to President Bush the way Mr de Valera did to Mr Churchill? Mr de Valera regarded the New Testament as the most serious document in history and he understood only too well that Mr Churchill, like Mr Bush, belonged to the Old Testament, not to the New Testament.

Tomorrow's Proclamation, Luke 2: 14, 'Glory to God in the highest, and on earth peace to men of good will.' What the sugar does that mean? What the Dickens can it mean?

I think that the Christmas Proclamation of peace is the most crucial document of history not because it is Christian but because it is true.

And it is an evolutionary truth, as well as an ethical truth. George W. Bush's war of terror against terror means that human evolution is now spiralling out of all solar hope, unravelling out of its own DNA. My anguish is my knowledge that the end of the world is at hand not because of some witchdoctor's prophecy but because of man's stupidity, greed, savagery, hypocrisy and our collective refusal to obey the laws of our own ethical nature.

Imagine being the leader of the most powerful country in the world and, in the hour of supreme crisis, ignoring your own ethical nature and, instead, grinning out of the corner of your mouth like a fifth-rate cowboy in a twelfth-rate Western B movie, 'Smoke 'em out, Jesus, smoke 'em out. Christ, child, we don't want no crummy, goddamn peace. Peace – why that's womenfolk's stuff. Smoke 'em out, boy, smoke 'em out.'

'Glory to King Herod in the highest, and on earth death to all women and children.'

'Spin Boldak is your only man.'

Silence. Silenzio. Ciúnas.

Peace. Pax. Suaimhneas.

The key word is the Irish word *suaimhneas*. Tonight about two thousand years ago saw the birth of *suaimhneas*; in the English, Sweet Peace. The mob rule of empire was confronted by the birth of the individual conscience in the person of a wandering, outcast, Palestinian Jew known to history as Christ.

Silence. Silenzio. Ciúnas. Peace. Pax. *Suaimhneas.*

December 24, 2001

SITTING AT MY MOTHER'S BEDSIDE

I've spent much of two weeks sitting at my mother's bedside in the orthopaedic ward of a public hospital.

She is eighty-six years old. Last summer she was well and bright and fragile. She and I spent a magical day sitting out in July sunlight in Palmerston Park. For the thirteen years since my father's death in January 1988 she has been living alone in an apartment overlooking Palmerston Park.

At summer's end she was admitted to a nursing home. Diagnosed, I was instructed, as having Alzheimer's disease. On the Thursday after Christmas Day she fell and broke her hip and on the Saturday she was operated on, the surgeon inserting a pin at the neck of the femur.

Sitting at Mummy's bedside, day in, day out, coming and going, I am aware that she too is coming and going: coming back to life, going out to death.

At first after the operation she appears to be going away forever. On the third day, the twigs of her jaws are clenched like a rabbit in a snare under the moon craters of her sealed eyes and I can see that she is marooned in a storm. But it blows over and next day she is sitting up in bed, still coming and going but not to the Antarctic of Death: coming and going to and from all the regions of her life, near and far, born Sheila MacBride, Westport, County Mayo, 1915.

The overwhelming storm over, I snooze at Mummy's bedside. Listening to and watching her coming and going. Listening to and watching myself coming and going. Listening to and watching the nurses and other patients coming and going. And all this is a mutual thing. Mummy too is enjoying watching the coming and going. Above all, she loves watching the sky outside – what she can glimpse of it. She is a small, spilt sea wooing moon.

She is in the bed furthest from the big window but the sky is her first and last preoccupation. The sky is the preoccupation of her days just as visiting her is the preoccupation of my days. Constantly she is scanning the ward window like a mariner with binoculars. Her grandfather Captain Patrick MacBride was a ship's captain from the Glens of Antrim and her father, Joseph MacBride, was Harbour Master in Westport. She croaks: 'There's a raininess up there but there's a nice piece of light and, look, there's another nice piece of light.'

She is in a ward on the first floor. I nip up the stairs instead of waiting for the lift. At the entrance to the ward I stop to salute a reproduction of Van Gogh's *Cafe Terrace At Night, Arles 1888*. Van Gogh, anything by Van Gogh, was always Mummy's favourite. She is criss-crossed by drips, transfusions, drains, bandages and an oxygen mask. I wait for her to notice me. Her thin, worn-out, eroded face lights up into a grin of amusement.

'What are you doing here?'

(Pause)

'Did you come in a *wheelchair*?'

(Pause)

'Your *purple* shirt! Looks well on you!'

(Pause)

'Your face – your face has got rounder.'

(She reaches out her hand – a long, bony, veiny articulation like the broken leg of a sheepdog.)

'Your face is not haggard anymore.'

(Pause)

'Get the wheelchair.'

(Pause)

'Where's the wheelchair?'

(Pause)

'*Succour* will come.'

(Pause)

'Your *purple* shirt!'

(Pause)

'Good old boy.'

(Pause)

'Get the wheelchair.'

(Pause)

'You're a Good Old Boy.'

(Pause)

'I must wash my *paws*.'

(Pause)

'What time is it?'

It is eleven o'clock in the morning. Ten minutes later Mummy starts reading my wristwatch upside down and she announces the time, accurately.

'Ten past eleven.'

(Pause)

'Belmullet is a long way.'

(Pause)

'The floodgates are going to open.'

(Pause)

'Where's the nearest loo?'

I rush out into the corridor and I find a young nurse who brings a commode. How amazing these young nurses are! Working thirteen-hour days for unjust wages and always so brave, so kind, so compassionate. She calls my mother 'Sheila' as all these young nurses do. Sheila! How wonderful to hear my mother called 'Sheila'.

Ten minutes later, Mummy is all neat, relaxed, shining, gleeful. She beams: 'Meet anyone fresh in Westport? Do you ever call around to old Patrick MacBride at the Quay? It's good to keep in touch. Are you going now?'

'I am, Mummy.'

'It'll do you good.'

She waves and, throwing back her head, she looks away from me in an air of detached contentment. On my way home, in the supermarket, at the shelves of juices, a prim lady in her sixties glances around at me and snaps: 'You are whistling into my right ear – stop it.'

Mummy always gives me a wave or even blows me a kiss when I leave her. She cries: 'Keep up the Bridge and come again. You can't come too often. Isn't that right?'

She blows a kiss in slow motion. She makes the sign of the cross, miming me a little papal blessing.

Next day it's Sunday January 6, the Feast of the Epiphany. As always, Mummy is amused to see me. She cries: 'Look – look at the sun! There! There! Behind that tree. Isn't it – isn't it? It's beautiful isn't it? I am going for a walk. Hold my hand. I won't dawdle. We mustn't dawdle.'

A priest wanders in and offers the Eucharist. I nod. He places it on her tongue and she drops her head and clasps her paws in embrace.

We have long silences too, Mummy and I, and I relish these silences. I close my eyes. After a long, long, blessedly long time Mummy asks: 'Are you tired? I've never seen you looking so tired. Your head is full of grey hairs.'

She smiles through her oxygen mask.

'I have a red dressing gown but it's too good to use so I keep it in the cupboard.'

We sit face to face, our chairs close, in silence, listening and watching. I chance a glance at Mummy. Her eyes are glistening out of her tangled, wet, blue-grey hair. Bending down she wipes her mouth with the hem of her blue nightie. She smiles. Then she lifts up her head sternly and gazes into the far distance – an eighty-six-year-old French Lieutenant's Woman gazing out to sea.

My poor, brave mother is a lighthouse in the fog of the cove of this wintry afternoon. I gaze over at her. Waiting for her to beam. Perched on her wispy crag, after twenty seconds, she beams.

She is so deaf I can hear her listening and then I can hear the wavelength she is on and I can hear the voice she is yearning for and leaning towards:

> *Lift up your eyes and look around:*
> *all are assembling and coming towards you,*
> *your sons from far away*
> *and daughters being carried at the hip*
>
> *At this sight you grow radiant,*
> *your heart throbbing and full …*

January 1, 2002

CAMP X-RAY

I want to talk this morning about what has been happening in Guantanamo Bay in Cuba these last three weeks but I am fearful of talking about it. Fearful? Fearful of what and whom? Fearful of the United States Government. As a citizen of what used be called the Civilised West, but has in Guantanamo Bay become the Barbarian West, I am as fearful of the current US Government as I used be of the KGB. There is now a McCarthyite climate of fear in which criticism of the US Government is deemed intolerable and inadmissible by that government.

Since I was five, when I saw my first Charlie Chaplin and Laurel and Hardy films, I have been a worshipper at the shrine of American culture, cinema, music, painting, history, sport and literature. I have had the good fortune to visit the US seven times: my beloved land of Muhammed Ali and the Harlem Globetrotters; of Jean Kennedy Smith and her fabled brothers; of Ella Fitzgerald, Marilyn Monroe and F. Scott

Fitzgerald; of Arthur Miller and Robert Zimmerman and Tiger Woods.

In 1961 the outstanding but obscure American Jesuit theologian John Courtney Murray appeared on the cover of *Time* magazine. Why? Because, as the author of a classic re-evaluation of the American Declaration of Independence – 'All men are created equal' – he entered the American Hall of Fame. I read that book in 1961 and I have consulted it many times since. It is entitled *We Hold These Truths*. 'We hold these truths to be self-evident ...' It is a book about the Natural Law and the American Constitution.

On barbarism he writes (p. 13): 'Barbarism is not, I repeat, the forest primeval with all its relatively simple savageries. Barbarism has long had its definition, resumed by St Thomas after Aristotle. It is the lack of reasonable conversation according to reasonable laws. Here the word "conversation" has its twofold Latin sense. It means living together and talking together.'

On war he writes (p. 255): 'All wars of aggression, whether just or unjust, fall under the ban of moral proscription.'

So it goes against the grain, against the American grain, against my own grain, to have to ask the question: is the one-year-old presidency of George W. Bush the gravest threat to western civilisation since the campaigns of the Soviet Union?

The policies of President Bush, from the declaration of the so-called 'War On Terrorism' to the current barbarism in Guantanamo Bay in Cuba, are the implementation of a tyranny which threatens the fundamental rights so humanely articulated by Benjamin Franklin and Thomas Jefferson and which undermines the ethos of the Founding Fathers – *compromise, compromise, compromise.*

And yet, neither the Irish nor the English media reflect the gravity of the crisis. Why? On top of universal fear of the US Government, our stupor may be due to journalists and commentators seeming to know history only in its eighteenth- to twentieth-century manifestations: that is, few seem to have any knowledge of medieval history, much less of the history of the Roman Empire.

George W. Bush is not a demon or an idiot. He is a young medieval warrior king drunk on power. And, as a reformed imbiber, his drunkenness is pure, undiluted. Or he is a young Roman Emperor in the fourth century AD, drunk not only on power but also on fear – his own fear of the great, dark migrations of Asiatic populations piling up on the northern and eastern frontiers of his empire.

The nightmare today is that the chipper young Emperor from Texas sees fit to scorn the Geneva Convention of 1949; sees fit to refuse to recognise POWs – prisoners of war; sees fit to maltreat and humiliate POWs in Afghanistan – shaving off their beards and crew-cutting their skulls before flying them twenty-seven hours shackled, manacled, leg-ironed, hooded, blindfolded, masked, gagged, ear-plugged in orange jumpsuits to a bare, barren, hot hole in south-east Cuba called Guantanamo, where the US has built a neo-space-age concentration camp which the US itself has officially christened 'Camp X-Ray'. There each animal – I mean prisoner – is incarcerated in a cage open to the elements, a cage of chain-link and a metal roof, a concrete floor and a mat.

The US Government has declared that these prisoner-animals have no legal rights. They will appear before military tribunals and, when found guilty, may be executed. The US Government and not the UN, the US Government and not God is the sole arbiter of right and wrong.

Meanwhile Ireland stands politely by while this week Minister Cowen visits China to chide, meekly-gruffly Tullamore-style, the Chinese on their human rights record and Bertie Ahern, Drumcondra-style, murmured niftily correct noises at a small gathering in Dublin last Thursday.

We Irish, as well as being terrified of the US Government, are a client of the US and, worse, we ourselves as a young democracy sold our soul to the US Government by prostrating ourselves in front of Clinton and Bush to give the credibility of the Oval Office, and the White House furniture in general, to the world's most successful terrorist organization – the IRA – and, finally, victory to the IRA in their Thirty Years War of terror against the Unionist population of the island of Ireland.

The Taliban and al Qaeda are terrorists. But the worst terror of all is the abolition by the USA of the rule of law in the name of democracy, in the hallowed names of Franklin and Jefferson.

I began these notes by recalling an American Jesuit priest, Fr John Courtney Murray, and I want to conclude by recalling another outstanding American priest Thomas Merton, the Cistercian monk who lived and worked all his life in the monastery of Gethsemane in Kentucky and who died, apparently by accidental electrocution, in 1968.

From the silence of his vows in the agony of his beloved Gethsemane, Thomas Merton lived out the 1960s protesting over and over and over again at the evil madness of the Vietnam War. One of the first poems I ever read in my life was a poem by Thomas Merton written for his brother who was a pilot in the US Air Force in World War Two. It is entitled: 'For My Brother: Reported Missing In Action, 1943' and it begins:

> *Sweet brother, if I do not sleep*
> *My eyes are flowers for your tomb;*
> *And if I cannot eat my bread,*
> *My fasts shall live like willows where you died.*
> *If in the heat I find no water for my thirst,*
> *My thirst shall turn to springs for you, poor traveller.*
>
> *Where, in what desolate and smoky country,*
> *Lies your poor body, lost and dead?*

And in what landscape of disaster
Has your unhappy spirit lost its road?

January 23, 2002

CHRISTMAS CARDS

The first week of February: time, I suppose, to take down the Christmas cards. Take down the Christmas cards? While all your neighbours in Irishtown, the far side of Ringsend Park in Stella Gardens, have been washed out of house and home by floods from the River Dodder, their cottages and cars and lives destroyed, you are talking about taking down your Christmas cards! Durcan, I knew you were a tulip but now I know you are *some* tulip.

Fair enough, but I'd be of no use to the good people of Stella because last week I slipped on the loose mat on the stair of my own cave, fell headlong to the bottom, burst my forehead and tore the wrist of my right hand, with the result that I cannot lift anything except cards.

So: time to take down the Christmas cards. Well, not take them *down*, as most of them were never *up* in the first place; no space in my cave except on top of a bookshelf and a mantel 3' by 30'. Most of the cards I've kept in piles on the floor, browsing them every other day, gazing at them, rejoicing in all the different images that different people choose, amazed at all the different charities, amazed too at the charity of those who sent me cards. No: time to put away the Christmas cards. I hate doing it but it has to be done.

I got two good months out of them. Soul-value.

Christmas cards: is there any more innocent form of affectionate communication, apart from a loving silence? Christmas cards are Expectation Vouchers.

The Christmas Expectation is a conundrum. I expect each Christmas to be the best ever, and always it transpires to be the worst ever. This Christmas was definitely the worst. Definitely.

And yet when each October comes around, what am I thinking? I'm thinking: Christmas is coming, there's light at the end of the tunnel: the crib, midnight mass, the Three Wise Men.

Let me try here not to be a hypocrite or, at least, if I cannot avoid hypocrisy (and maybe it is impossible for a human to avoid hypocrisy – hypocrisy is our situation, our human predicament), let me claim to be a happy hypocrite and say that while the Christian fairytale of Christmas is crucially important to me, so too is the Santa Claus story of Christmas.

Christmas is not only a co-production between Christ and Santa Claus; the Christmas Expectation goes far beyond the birth of Christ and the chimney rock-climbing of Santa Claus. Christmas, all in all, constitutes some far greater kind of expectation, some sort of supreme poetry which finds its elemental expression in the form of the Christmas card.

The clock of expectation began ticking in October. It's what got us through October and November. In my case I published a book called *Cries of an Irish Caveman* and I spent all of October and November going up and down and around Ireland and England giving poetry readings. From Balbriggan to the Barbican in London (Balbriggan won hands down);

from Cork City to Eton College (Eton College won hands down; Cork City never liked me – *yerra boy, but we cut you down to size, didn't we? In fact, that's why Cork city was invented; to cut tinkers like you, Durcan, down to size*).

The first Christmas card to arrive every year arrives in the first week of December from Fr Patrick O'Brien of Claremorris, Co. Mayo. It is always a Xeroxed A-4 page folded in two with printed images and texts; this year a Zen painting by Thomas Merton and poems by Merton and Daniel Berrigan and Patrick O'Brien along with two letters from Fr O'Brien himself, one printed 'Dearest Friends', one handwritten 'Dearest Paul'. He writes: 'Can we imagine Christ with a knife, a sword, a bomb?' I cherish Fr O'Brien's Christmas card more than I can ever say and look forward to it with all my heart every year.

Then, like Tennyson's *Brook*, a trickle becomes a little mountain stream of Christmas cards hurrying through the lips of my letterbox, slipping, fretting, sliding, lingering, loitering, chattering.

'For men may come and men may go
But Christmas cards go on for ever.'

And our kindly Ringsend postman Pat Corri goes on from door to door, whose ancestors came from Mount Street and, before Mount Street, from Italy's reddest shores.

Three cards which, like Fr Patrick O'Brien's card, if any failed to arrive I'd go into jumping-into-the-river mode: one from Jane and Tony with always a letter from Jane with the latest news about her amazing man and on the card a painting or drawing by her – this Christmas it's called 'Meadow Flowers'; second, a card from Edna and Michael with always a drawing of her father's soul by their daughter Sarah; and third, a card called 'Skaters' – Dutch folk on ice – from my eremite friend at the Merrion Gates, James Springfield.

A card depicting 'Snow On Croagh Patrick' as painted by Tom Smith for CROI – West of Ireland Cardiology

Foundation from my cousin in Westport, Mary MacBride Walsh.

An Oxfam Card from Laura Lake in Co. Leitrim with a redheaded angel blowing a golden trumpet over a medieval roof-scape with palm trees. Laura Lake! *Hic transit* Gloria Swanson – and Laura Lake!

A card from Lanzarotte from the Lanzarotte Two containing the handwritten first lines of a new song based on Brother Moore's 'Lisdoonvarna':

Oh Lanzarotte!

Lanzar, Lanzar Lanzar, Lanzarotte!

'The Procession of the Red Deer Stags' with love from Jane O'Briain of Scurlock's Leap.

From Pádraic Carr – the architect of Achill Island – and his Lorraine and little Patrick, the Dove of Peace with holly in its beak.

A card from one Rosie Joyce from whom I've never had a Christmas card before, for the simple reason that last Christmas she was only three months in her mother's womb. But this Christmas she is seven months old. Her card is a black ink drawing of her – a perfect likeness. Black boots, tartan skirt, tunic top with frilly collar and a pair of eyes that would telescope you dead-alive at a distance of ten thousand light years.

From Monaseed of the Berneys (the Donal McCann Berneys), a different CROI card designed by my namesake in Galway, Mel Durkan; Durkan with a 'K'. A 'K' Durcan. As opposed to a 'C' Durcan.

From the Big Mountain in Achill Island – Three Shepherds from Mary Hoban in aid of the Lifeboat Service of Ireland.

A solitary ewe between two bare trees – from all at the Poets House, Falcarragh, Co. Donegal – Janice Simmons.

From a Senior Archivist in the National Archives, on a piece of handmade paper, a coloured-ink painting by O'Faolain.

From Conor, Vona, Tommy and Eve, a Sculpture in Blue in aid of St Joseph's School For Blind Boys.

From the Great Flynn of Clifden Arts Week – Rudolph the Red-nosed Reindeer in aid of the Galway Hospice Foundation.

'Billy Brennan's Barn' from Tony and Rachel in Galway. 'The bicycles go by in twos and threes … There's a dance in Billy Brennan's Barn tonight.' Produced by the Patrick Kavanagh Rural and Literary Resource Centre in Inniskeen, Co. Monaghan.

From Futoshi Sakauchi of Tokyo, Japan – the Three Wise Men.

From Síabhra and Blaise in the fields of Ballymahon, Co. Longford, a print made by themselves of men in black pointy hats sliding down Mont Blanc in 1827. *Glissading*, Monsieur. (Copyright: Royal Geographical Society, London.)

From Mr Michael Carr of Dookinella and his daughter Ann and her husband Pauric Corrigan, a boiled fruit cake in a red-tin sweet box. My God, am I not blest?

From Carrie of the heart as big as Waterford – 'Wishing you lots of "good madness".' Oxfam.

From Mary Banotti MEP – a bunch of Afghan women in burkas with a little, barefaced, bright-eyed girl peeping out of the middle of the front row.

'We wish you a Happy Cave Christmas' – Mary, Niall and Catherine. Oxfam.

A Cystic Fibrosis Association card from Auntie Vi of the one, the only Gray's Guest House in the village of Dugort in Achill Island.

From the lovely lady who, after ten winters together, broke my heart, a painting of 'Snowdrops' by Sarah Summers. In aid of the Leonard Cheshire Homes with the logo 'Supporting charity, radiating quality'.

'The Mountains of Korea' by Dong Chun Lee from courageous, indomitable, mega-magnanimous Dorothy Walker.

'We found juniper berries in Henaghan's of Castlebar. Hope lives.' Sheila, Brent and Conor. 'Christmas Garden' by Graffiti.

'To Paul From Sky' – that's young Sky McCracken Aughey from her beloved Belfast.

From dearest, bravest and most betrayed of Irishmen by Irishmen, Brian Kennedy in Canberra, Australia, a characteristically optimistic but defiant message on a card by the great Aboriginal painter Rover Thomas called 'All that big rain coming from top side'.

First and last, a card from the Inishowen peninsula which I'll keep up on my mantel: a Christmas wreath with the message – 'Love from us both. P.S. Hope you get through the Christmas okay. B.'

That's not even the half of them. I'd be here until that singing-bird newscaster Sean O'Rourke comes on at 1 p.m. if I was to go through them all and, besides, they bring on a sadness, don't they? That's the rub, the funny elbow of Christmas; it's a suspension bridge that's riveted with so many aspirations that it's all too much. Christmas is unbearable because it highlights like nothing else our earthly loneliness.

Nothing for it now but to dream of next Christmas – of Egypt, maybe even of Mayo.

February 6, 2002

THE MILLENNIUM WING OF
THE NATIONAL GALLERY

The second week of February and of springtime – time to go into town and visit the new Millennium Wing of the National Gallery of Ireland which opened its doors only three weeks ago. The entrance to the original gallery remains on Merrion Square but now there is a second grand entrance on Clare Street, where four rivers converge: Clare Street, South Leinster Street, Lincoln Place, Nassau Street.

What an exhilarating day! I wake up feeling grim; I could not sleep half the night, craving only to stay in the sack. But by 10.30 a.m. I am walking east along Clare Street past Greene's bookshop. I cat-leap across the street so as to approach the new Millennium Wing from the far side and behold the new entrance. What the architects have done – Gordon Benson and Jim Hutcheson from Glasgow and Alan Forsyth from Tyneside (what eyesight they must have, these Scots and the Northumbrian!) – they have broken through from Merrion Square into Clare Street, opening up a brand-new entrance equal to and as beautiful as the original portico entrance. This new façade is like the best of modern church architecture – Liam McCormick updated; its plain, floating walls of white Portland Stone sink into the streetscape – the Georgian vista of Nassau Street, the high palings of Trinity, the red-brick Finn's Hotel where Nora Barnacle was chambermaiding when she first bumped into her James Joyce on Nassau Street in 1904.

It's a dark, gusty morning with blobs of rain ballooning in the air. I skate in the door and find myself in a lit-up, south-lit, aspiring universe of lots and lots of people busy at social intercourse. Where am I? It feels like at once a shopping centre, a cathedral and a theatre. (In future in Ireland, all shopping centre, church and theatre architects should be dragged screeching to the Millennium Wing to learn what architecture is really all about.)

The box-office is a stage-set or, I should say, the Information Desk, for it is always important to say and say again that ADMISSION IS FREE into the National Gallery of Ireland. This is one of the few practical freedoms of our democratic republic. The National Gallery is as much a venue for coffee or lunch or resting your feet and people-watching or buying a book or a card or just strolling about doing nothing as it is a picture gallery. The only time you ever pay to see pictures in the National Gallery is for a special visiting exhibition such as the current Impressionist Show, which has travelled from Boston to celebrate the first flight of the Millennium Wing, which itself constitutes the fourth wing of the National Gallery – the other wings being the Beit Wing, the Dargan and the Milltown. 'A gallery never flew on one wing!' 'Yes, Ma'am.'

The Information Desk is the first of many theatres I will encounter today. The new wing is a matryoshka doll of theatre within theatre within theatre. The Information Desk is a free-standing black box. I leave my coat and bag in the cloakroom – and I'm hopping that even the cloakroom is yet another small theatre! Its counter is a seductive double-S shape of ash timber painted black. Behind the counter, two affable attendants. The attendants in the National Gallery of Ireland are the girders of it all.

Making a beeline for the Coffee Bar I climb a flight of Portland Stone steps. The Coffee Bar – yet another theatre – is itself as congenial as the excellent café latté which I order from a young man from Northern China. I say to him: 'Coffee is bad for you.' He smiles shut-eyed and murmurs: 'In China we drink tea.' After a gulp of coffee, it dawns on me that I've only been in the new Millennium Wing thirty minutes and I already feel like a whole day has passed. This Coffee Bar is a side-altar of a medieval cathedral in the heart of a medieval village, all kind and manner and age and class of people coming and going. The black woman in a white overcoat at the table next me has painted her nails green.

But what is creating all this 'buzz and atmo' is the actual building itself.

I've been in many galleries around the world but I have never seen the like of this new Millennium Wing. The National Gallery of Ireland has become also the Inter-National Gallery of Ireland.

It's all angles and vast unpainted plaster walls out of which suddenly pop – and pop back – faces. You look up and the wall is blank. You look up again and a face is peering out at you. It's all apertures and nooks. On the top floor overlooking Clare Street there is a niche with a built-in seat for two. Many is the marriage that will be consummated or, at least, made here.

The Millennium Wing is like living inside a medieval painting. It's like the Irish back line in the rugby match against Wales, all the walls and staircases running at different angles to one another. The Millennium Wing is all Brian O'Driscoll and Kevin Maggs and Geordan Murphy; all running across one another's flight paths and therefore all of them crashing over the Welsh line for score after score after score.

Reluctantly I depart the Coffee Bar. It is so tasteful and inviting; the work of the Finnish architect Alvar Aalto but provided by O'Hagan Design here in Dublin. The tables are of blond birch and the chairs are blond birch frames with black canvas webbing.

Back outside the Coffee Bar is the crossroads, the hub. You can either turn right and stroll into the old gallery or you can turn left into the new Modern Irish Art gallery or you can cross opposite to the Donation Wall in which are carved in Portland Stone, by the English stone carver Richard Kindersley, the names of the Benefactors, Carmel and Martin Naughton, Margery and Alastair McGuckian, Sir Anthony and Lady O'Reilly. Let me hear no tittering at the back of the class; without the gratuitous generosity of these patrons there would be no Millennium Wing. I turn right and head up the next staircase to the Impressionist Show.

All the greats are there – Van Gogh, Cézanne, Monet, Renoir, Degas. There is a little Degas oil to melt your cold little soul, entitled *At the Races in the Countryside, 1869*. The middle-class husband in topper driving his horse and carriage, in which his wife sits watching a wet-nurse breast-feeding their baby, a splash of pink over the left black blinker of the horse. But it is the works of painters I've never heard of that grab me by the toes – especially in the last section. *Cottage in the Dunes* by Cazin: pure Andrew Wyeth, pure Edward Hopper. Or Dagnan-Bouveret's *Willows by a Stream 1908*. (By the way, quite a few visitors seemed to be missing out on the last section. Remember – you have to cross the bridge to see the last section.)

The bridge! From which you can gaze down into what was the Georgian garden of 5 South Leinster Street and is now the Winter Garden restaurant, the far wall of which is the retained rear of Number 5 in all its Georgian bays and on the inner side of which is the freestanding Regency Ballroom. Or from the other side of the bridge you can gaze down into the entrance area far below and run your eyes up and down the floor-to-skylight Aubusson tapestry by Louis Le Brocquy. Entitled *The Death Of Cúchullain*, it's all balls; all coloured balls.

Three hours later I feel I am entitled to a second visit to the Coffee Bar – this time for an apple juice and a sanger.

The paintings I have seen, and the people I have bumped into, dance and die, die and dance in my mind. I meet a lady from Limerick, Pauline Purcell, up by train for the day to visit the Millennium Wing. I crash into John Twin MacNamara from Dooagh on Achill Island with his daughter Damhnait. We have a brief but big laugh. Michael Cullen – the magic painter – waves from the Winter Garden restaurant on the ground floor across the mall from the bookshop. Michael is in a daze like myself. He is admiring the open-heart old brickwork of the ballroom. Joseph Brennan whom I first met twenty-one years ago in the Boulevard Montparnasse in the apartment of Madame Levanthal. Today he is accompanying Lady Beit who has come to look at *her* wing – the Beit wing. Lady Beit is wearing gleaming red slippers like the young Noll Gogarty in Orpen's fantabulous portrait in the Orpen Chapel in the new Modern Irish Art gallery, and she is leaning on a green umbrella – an eighteenth-century shade of green. Jean Tansey, filmmaker, also in a trance, in white and red, drifting purposefully.

Exiting from the Impressionist Show, Dorothy and Pádraig Flynn – the mighty Flynn whom I last met sixteen years ago on the desolate side of a bare mountain in a rainstorm in the County of Mayo: the opening of Knock International Airport in May 1986. I find him now as I found him then, a man of passionate courtesy, a man of gay defiance. Back then in Knock in 1986 he held high his head when all the Dublin economists and calculators – except for

Charles Haughey and Monsignor Horan – scoffed at the 'boggy' airport.

He tells me a story against myself. How audacious of him! Nothing like having the bottom of one's own bottomless vanity blown out of the water.

'Anyways,' he says, 'how are you?'

I mutter something about 'vicissitudes'.

'Ah the Vicissitudes,' he sings to me, peering down from the windswept mountaintop of that high head of his, 'the Vicissitudes!'

And he sings on: 'The Vicissitudes! The Vicissitudes! The Vicissitudes are what make life worth living.'

February 13, 2002

BACK TO THE NATIONAL GALLERY

What else is a National Gallery for but for going back to, again and again – and ADMISSION FREE except for the Impressionist Show. Not only has our National Gallery given birth to its Millennium Wing but also the old gallery has been re-designed, re-hung with many pictures not shown before and newly wallpapered.

At 10.20 a.m. I swing left off Fenian Street into Merrion Street only to be halted by a vista of traffic cones on both sides of the street outside the National Gallery. Gardaí in yellow hi-viz jackets everywhere. Don't panic Durcan, and I don't, and I find space on the south side of Merrion Square. I walk down to Clare Street to enter by the new Millennium Wing. More Gardaí. I ask: 'Who is all this for?' A young Garda smiles: 'Prince Charles.'

At the cloakroom the genial attendant is hollering after a small man: 'You've forgot your number, sir.' 'Oh,' exclaims the small man, 'it's the pure excitement of it all.' At the foot of the new staircase of Portland Stone stand, sentinel to the coming Prince, two square terracotta pots painted pewter grey with ten-foot-high slender trunks wrapped in moss and each topped with a bouquet of yellow roses, white roses, orchids and sprays of fern and grasses. Another pair stand sentinel at the top of the stairs.

I nip into the Coffee Bar, gasping for a latté. The Director of the National Gallery, Raymond Keaveney, is knocking back a cuppa. He laughs and hasn't he every right to? He of 'the broad mind' – to quote Ciarán Lennon's phrase – for it was Raymond Keaveney whose original idea the Millennium Wing was when he was appointed in 1988. His very first proposal as Director was to build the Millennium Wing. In 1990 Brian P. Kennedy was appointed Assistant Director and the National Gallery entered the space age with Messrs Keaveney and Kennedy firing off the rockets and the fireworks with the help of a premier-league staff: Marie Bourke, Head of Education, curators Fionnuala Croke, Sergio Benedetti and Adrian le Harivel; and Maureen Ryan, the dedicated, gracious Director of the Friends of the National Gallery.

Today Raymond Keaveney has a few appointments: 11 a.m., Bertie Ahern; 12 noon, Board Meeting; 3 p.m., Prince Charles; 4.30 p.m., reception to mark the end of the Board Chairman Carmel Naughton's six-and-a-half-year term of office. Leaving the Coffee Bar I turn left at the crossroads for the new Modern Irish Art Gallery – admission free. Apart from the new Orpen Chapel, the pictures I fancy are: Grace Henry's *Misty Moonlight*, 1912 – a tiny picture, maybe 12' by 10', of Achill Island, almost abstract; Daniel O'Neill's *Early Morning* and *Scarecrows in Newtownards* – O'Neill was the Matisse with a dash of Modigliani of twentieth-century Irish art: sumptuous, ominous; Patrick Collins's *Liffey Quaysides* – Collins was Howard Hodgkin before Howard Hodgkin became Howard Hodgkin – that Collins nimbus enclosing the Liffey; Colin Middleton's *Fish and Chipper* – a very

Millennium Wing streetscape, all gables and cul-de-sacs with a discreet RC church offstage. I remark to an attendant that the Middleton has no label. 'Ah,' he says, 'we might put a label on it for you in the next millennium.' Harry Kernoff's *David Byrne's pub 1941* as painted from the Bailey; odd that it's not called Davy Byrne's as it is nowadays and was in Joycetime. Le Brocquy's *The Family*, 1951 – you can see Picasso, Moore, Bacon at the front of Le Brocquy's mind but it is in his own voice, and the mother looks very like Le Brocquy himself. I eavesdrop on the curator Síle Breathnach-Lynch's talk to the Friends of the National Gallery. Living artists can never be part of the permanent collection of the National Gallery but she tells us how she went to the Board and said that she had to hang le Brocquy: 'I said to the Board – Le Brocquy is a great Irish artist who's managed to keep himself alive, please let me hang him.' Permission was granted and so she hung le Brocquy. The showstopper is Patrick Tuohy's portrait of *Biddy Campbell, 1930*. Against blue, she looks sideways out in pink chequered mini-dress, long bare legs, beribboned sunhat. 'Biddy Campbell – the Pride of the Wing! The Mill-En-I-Um Humming Wing!' That's a song I got in the Coffee Bar from a fair-haired young man in a snazzy, black leather jacket.

What a grand pilgrimage it is to walk the short, slow, silent passage from the Millennium Wing into the old gallery. You pass into the old – old! – atrium opened only in 1996. Such stillness. The Millennium Wing has given new life to Felim Egan's *Four Seasons* in the atrium. Now it can be called the 'Egan Atrium'.

I enter the Milltown Wing, newly wallpapered in eighteenth-century green – Sutcliffe green – and re-hung by Síle Breathnach-Lynch. She has created what amounts to a Thomas Roberts Room – he of the landscapes of Lucan, Clonskeagh, Ballyshanon and Belleek. In another room she has installed a huge Venus and opposite it the huge Adam and

Eve by James Barry. A leaf of the apple serves as the most subtle fig leaf you have ever seen.

I proceed into the Dargan Wing and through the George Bernard Shaw Cathedral into the Yeats Chapel and say a prayer to Papa John Yeats and a salute to Jack, Lily and Lolly (and to the family curator, Hilary Pyle). Up the steps into and through the startling new Room 20 back into the Milltown Wing and Frank O'Meara's girl in moon mist so magnanimously loaned by its recent purchaser. I say 'the startling new Room 20'. This is a passing-through room for contemporary Irish artists to exhibit in. Ciarán Lennon has four large paintings all about colour, inspired by Cézanne colour and Poussin colour. Lennon also offers us a fascinating catalogue for the throwaway price of €4. I cross over into the Beit Wing, also newly wallpapered by its curator Adrian Le Harivel – a sort of ochre colour except that it is not ochre. It is a shade of golden ochre called 'wet sands'. How about that! Wet Sands! Next time you're wallpapering, try out 'wet sands'.

In the last room of the Beit Wing I come upon yet another new exhibition, curated by Adrian Le Harivel, called 'The Monarch's Head' – a sequence of monarch's heads from Queen Elizabeth I through Charles I, culminating in a series of portraits of the Prince Regent and later George IV, he whose mistress lived in Slane – which is why the Finglas-Slane road is as straight as a rod. I find a crowd of visitors listening, watching, laughing and – hey – here is a Royal lecturing on his ancestors. Can it, could it be – Prince Charles? No – it's not Charles, it's actually the Prince Regent himself, later George IV, and he is skipping about telling us the most scandalous gossip but sprinkled with gems of the finest art-historical erudition and I cannot help but observe that the high-boned, red-cheeked Prince bears more than a passing resemblance to Adrian Le Harivel.

Of the life-size statue of his father, George III, he tells us '… and then my poor father stood in the car park of the Point

Theatre for eight years directing traffic until the Corporation agreed to loan him to the National Gallery'. Of Turner de Lond's huge canvas of himself – *The Public Entry of George IV into Dublin, 17th August 1821*, he tells us: 'I have to say that I looked very elegant that day. I always take pride in the right clothes for the right occasion.' Of the magnificent Thomas Lawrence portrait of himself (on loan from the Mansion House), he drawls 'One of the greatest painters of myself.' This *tour-de-force* one-man show at 10.30 a.m., worthy of the Gate Theatre on an exceptionally good night, has been organised by Maureen Ryan for the Friends of the National Gallery.

Anyone can become a Friend for only €50 (concessions €35). There are benefits including daily access to the home of the Friends, 90 Merrion Square, built in 1750 and former home of the great orthopaedic surgeon Mr Arthur Chance and his protégé Dr Noel Browne. Frank McDonald's felicitous phrase about the Millennium Wing is true also of the old gallery: it has 'a clarity of circulation'. I stroll back through Egan's Atrium, down the grand new staircase and into the brand-new National Gallery bookshop.

Spacious on a humane scale, the shop is managed by the indomitable Marie FitzGerald, formerly of Waterstones, Hodges Figgis, Books Unlimited Donaghmede, Menzies Edinburgh and Easons. Along with Ruth Kenny of Books Upstairs she has long been by repute one of the two Crown Princesses of the Irish book trade. The new National Gallery bookshop is now among the best art bookshops in Ireland.

Upstairs Prince Charles has arrived to visit the Millennium Wing but, unfortunately, he has entered through the old Merrion Square entrance. To appreciate the kind of building the Millennium Wing is, one simply *must* enter by the new Millennium entrance on Clare Street. The Prince – a decent chap by all accounts – is mystified when on crossing over the great new bridge in the Millennium Wing it is pointed out to him that from the bridge you can actually see the street outside. 'But, but ...' he cries in a slightly-strangled-by-laryngitis voice, 'surely if you want to see the street outside, you jolly well stay out on the street.' Prince Charles expresses himself charmed by the Renoirs but perhaps his visit is all slightly too hasty because Rule Number One about the National Gallery of Ireland is that you must give it time. The point about pictures, as about books or going to the zoo, is that in the company of pictures and books and wild creatures time stands still. Outside, the pink sun is beginning to go down into the Phoenix Park and on each gate into Merrion Square there is a sign which says: *Please shut this gate gently.*

February 19, 2002

THE REFERENDUM BLUES

The Sunday before last, the first Sunday in Lent, I found myself sitting at the same table as a beautiful woman in her forties from County Kerry with golden curly hair and red cheeks, and her smile was the coral-pink sun of nightfall on a summer's night going down into the western ocean.

We chatted on and off for three hours about lots of things under the sun and then we stood up to go our different ways. I asked her how she was feeling about the Referendum. Almost as if I had made to assault her, she put her hands up to her ears. Fiercely, she whispered: 'They are not going to drag me down for a third time; I will listen to none of it but on the day I will go there and vote No, No, No!'

No more mature, conscientious, warm-hearted, charitable, imaginative, sane woman could you meet. Since meeting her that last Sunday before Lent, I have made a point of asking other sane, conscientious women how they feel, and from every woman the response has been the same:

one of anguish and anger – angry anguish – and a resolve not to allow the public voices wailing, bickering, nattering on either side to invade her privacy; a determination to carry on with her life and all the day-to-day difficulties that daily life entails and not to allow the weighing-scales of her soul to be spilled by gusts of hysteria or by boorish rhetoric or by icy formulations of lawyers and doctors or by the antics of politicians in what she and so many women perceive as an atmosphere of cruelty and ignorance. One woman winced: 'I don't want loads of men running up and down my fallopian tubes.'

(Ignorance! I checked with my own two local post offices to see how many people had asked for their free copy of the Referendum Bill: one from each post office. One! And one of those ones was my own little self!)

Word for word, gesture for gesture, the Kerry woman's response mirrored my own response. From the outset I have tried not to listen, not to watch, not to read, praying that my life would not be invaded and polluted once again. I dread the so-called Abortion Referendums for the bad atmosphere they create: the bad language; the bad faith; the bad manners.

Yet of course it is impossible to withstand the assault on one's soul and the bad atmosphere that is created every time in Ireland we have a referendum touching on sexuality.

This pollution was epitomised on Ash Wednesday, February 13, when the Taoiseach, black ashes on his forehead, stood up in the Dáil like a prizefighter and traded blows with the Opposition while, all round the House, deputies howled at one another. I felt like a terrified child watching my parents quarrelling.

Why does the subject of what is called 'abortion' lead to such malevolence, hysteria, stupidity, bad manners? I say 'what is called "abortion"' because the very word itself has been so abused as to have become, in humane discourse, unusable. Misuse and abuse of language seem a necessary part of Abortion Referendums.

> *I got the Referendum Blues;*
> *So what's news?*
> *Daffodils in queues;*
> *I got the Referendum Blues;*
> *I got the Referendum Blues.*

I have the feeling that we humans are terrified of facing up to the three basic mysteries of existence: birth, sex and death.

Take death. In thirty years of murder and massacre in Ireland, what leader of Church or State, what leader of anything, has ever come before us and done a Martin Luther King and stated the absolute unacceptability of so much as one political murder ever, ever, under any circumstances? Instead, bishops and primates and politicians ritually condemned each and every murder and stated what an atrocious tragedy it was; and such was the repetition of this mantra that frequently the poor family of the murdered one would bleat: 'If our poor Johnny's death helps to bring peace, he will not have died in vain.'

In reality – but we don't much like reality, do we? – we should never have accepted one single political murder, not because it is wrong, which it is, but because it is fundamentally anti-social, an abuse of human beings as intolerable as the abuse of children.

In the early 1970s the leaders of Church and State should have shed respectability and taken to living in the streets themselves, camping like eco-warriors outside the offices of the IRA and the British Army and the UDA and, by dint of speaking only in natural silence and natural language, made it impossible for the blue eyes of militarism and the kiss-curls of terrorism to blackmail us anymore. But no: death is not something we want to face up to, then or now.

Likewise our attitudes to old age, disability and homelessness. We who once treated the elders of the tribe with reverence and awe, now we mock them with cold neglect. As one church-going solicitor once roared at me: 'You can sleep in doorways all you like but not in my doorway.' Nor is birth something we want to face up to seriously. Do we feel that Death and Birth are too serious to be taken seriously? Instead, like very primitive animals, we surround Death and Birth with all sorts of screens and taboos and rituals and laws; all done in order to avoid facing reality.

Despite our technology we have become more superstitious, more ignorant, more callous and more afraid of reality than our prehistoric ancestors. The very few wise people we have in our society – like John McGahern or John Moriarty or the late Iris Murdoch – we ignore what they have to say to us.

Sadly, it is not really surprising that these Abortion Referendums bring out the worst in us. We cannot face death truthfully; therefore how can we expect ourselves to face sexuality and birth truthfully, modestly, humbly?

Is the Abortion Referendum a black joke, the blackest of red herrings? All vanity, all hubris? The real question is: do we have any values as a society – a specific huddle of humans on a tiny island off the north-west coast of Europe? And if we do have any values as a social entity, what are these values? Rather than think about such questions, our rulers amuse themselves and distract us with tribunals and referendums.

The holding of the current referendum – the way it has been produced, staged and directed – would suggest to a Martian that Ireland, as a social entity, has no values when it comes to questions of life and death, all of which are interrelated and no one of which can be isolated from the other.

Terrified of the truth about sexuality and birth, we hide behind the furniture of political games.

Why?

I think it is because Man – the male of the species – especially the Irish male of the species – is more afraid of life than of death. He is scared of death but he is terrified of life and so, in practical terms of the Abortion Referendum, man is terrified of woman and, therefore, seeks to control woman as much as he can. For as long as man has existed, man has sought to dominate and control birth and, therefore, woman. From the witch-doctors of prehistory to the lawyers of today, the primeval urge is the same: to control the means and methods of birth at all costs. Therefore, in politics, man cannot allow woman freedom of conscience when it comes to her role as mother. Likewise, in religion, man cannot allow woman to become a priest. Even on its own terms the Referendum Black Charade is just that – a Black Charade. Since the foundation of the State no Irish Government has been willing to provide proper and adequate health services or proper and adequate education, least of all the governments in the richest years of the State. So it is that the wide range of caring services that should be available to all the women of Ireland simply do not exist.

Such has been the eighty-odd-years schizoid mentality of the State that it can actually be brazen enough to propose Abortion Referendums while at the same time never providing proper and adequate health and care services for women.

I walk the streets and the quays at lighting-up time. Every lamppost under pink sodium light has a poster, like a headless chicken impaled, dumbly screaming at me. I pass my local church with its beautiful east window of Mary trailing a vast cloak of blue. Often I nip into the church for peace of mind but not today. Today only the sky and the wind and the river offer peace of mind.

> *I got the Referendum Blues;*
> *So what's news?*

Daffodils in queues;
I got the Referendum Blues;
I got the Referendum Blues.

February 26, 2002

ROSIE JOYCE

Eight months ago my daughter Sarah and her husband, Mark Joyce, gave birth to a baby girl whom they named and christened Rosie – Rosie Joyce.

This last winter the two big things in my life have been driving over to the North Side of Dublin to the secret back streets up behind the Broadstone and getting to take Rosie Joyce out for a walk, or driving south to the outskirts of the city to visit my eighty-six-year-old mother in the nursing home where she is courageously drifting out to sea on tides of old age, in gales of Alzheimer's, but crewed with nurses of hearts of gold.

When Rosie Joyce was born in May last year, mischief makers were only too quick to exclaim to me: 'So you are a grandfather now?' While I stammered and blushed and hummed and hawed they'd repeat, nice and easy and slowly and gleefully: 'So you're a grandfather now!'

On the other hand, I'm only too delighted to report, too vain to report, that I have been mistaken for her father. Oh yes!

On a damp, blue-grey, mild January morning in St Stephen's Green, beside the pond, a young Asian lady takes a delicate but massive shine to Rosie. She bends down like a big, sleek mother pigeon and coos at Rosie. 'May I?' she asks me. 'O yes, yes,' I reply, puffing out my forehead like a superior mother; a mother superior with knobs on. And she lifts up Rosie in her arms high above her head like the priest raising the host. An Asian priestess in a three-quarter-length black leather coat. She sits down beside me with Rosie on her knee. She inquires of me, ever so gently, tentatively: 'What – what is your relation with baby?'

I pretend not to understand.

'This baby – your baby?'

Again I beam like an idiot.

'Father of baby – you?'

I shake my head.

'Ah – you – grandfather to baby?'

She laughs and asks: 'Is it usual in Ireland for grandfather to look after baby?'

'Oh yes,' I reply, looking around me helplessly searching for all the grandfathers of Ireland minding all the babies of Ireland.

We sit in an easy silence, admiring Rosie in her mustard woolly hat with, knitted to its sides, a ladybird in red, a hedgehog in brown, a mouse in grey and a bee in yellow and black. Rosie is laughing. I've never known a baby to laugh so much. The Asian lady tells me she herself is from Korea.

'Are you from Seoul?' I ask her showing off my incredible knowledge of geography.

'No, I from Pusan,' she tells me, putting me in my place. (It's only when I get back to my cave in Ringsend and consult my *Times Atlas* that I find Pusan; a port city on the south-east shores of Korea facing Japan.)

I push Rosie along past the O'Donovan Rossa boulder into Grafton Street. At the carnival display of flower sellers at the mouth of Harry Street I buy two bunches of tulips and then boldly – oh so boldly – ask a flower seller if she'd mind taking a photo of me and Rosie. The flower seller throws me a knowing, possibly critical look and grabs my camera. After she takes the snap, I cannot help boasting to her about my baby. I cry out: 'Her name is Rosie!' while at the same time throwing the stalls of roses an emphatically casual glance. The weather-beaten flower seller offers me a shoot of a smile.

Our most regular port of call, mine and Rosie's, is the National Botanic Gardens in Glasnevin. Even in the dead of winter the Botanic Gardens is one of the most beautiful Gardens on earth. I have had the good fortune to have visited some other far-flung Gardens in Brazil and in Madeira and in Batumi on the Black Sea in Georgia and in Kyoto in Japan and our Botanics are as beautiful.

I call for Rosie up behind the Broadstone. Her Dad or her Mum install her in a car seat in the back of the car and I'm away. The trouble – my trouble – starts when at the Gardens I try to unpack Rosie. Being a twenty-first-century baby is like being an astronaut on long-haul duty up in a space station for two or three years. Constantly being trussed up and strapped in; constantly being transferred from one confined space to another; from car seat to baby buggy; from high chair to cot. I make a poor co-pilot for you, Rosie. Struggling to unpack the buggy and then to re-assemble it, I cannot figure out all the straps and bars – it's all a kind of space-age Lego – so in the end I have to improvise and let things hang out a little loosely. Rosie is happy as Rosie, but what would her parents say?

In a dark drizzle, we head off around the borders of the gardens. We come upon clumps of young men and young women digging and cutting and transplanting. How I envy them! How I'd love to have been a gardener! And I glimpse a fleeting image of my younger daughter Síabhra in County

Longford in her garden by the River Tang or in her bed in the trees reading *The Botany of Desire* by Michael Pollan.

I keep up a running monologue with Rosie. A half-running, half-walking monologue with many a stop to identify a tree or a shrub. Rosie puts up with all of this with a calm, merciful, papal countenance or with quick, brief sonatas of merriment. She loves to laugh. She builds up a great head of laughter until it becomes a mountain torrent in spate. She builds up from diminuendo to crescendo and she opens her mouth wide as wide can be to display her two little teeth sprouting in the centre seats in the bottom front row and her mouth gets opened wider than Pavarotti's on a climax.

Today she's wearing her pink space suit with rabbit ears.

Happiness. This is happiness for which, God be praised, there are no words, and which of its essence is utterly transient.

Down at the mill race, I realise that we've been two hours on the go. Time to head back to the car-park. As with many a pant I push Rosie up the hill along the Yew Walk, I cross paths with a trio of young housewives in brightly coloured raincoats with buggies. As soon as they set eyes on me, they all break into laughter. What a stunning housewife I make in my long, navy-blue, heavy overcoat and white trainers, my gasping white face under a coming-apart thatch of grey hair.

Still, it is I who lead the way up the Yew Walk with the three young female housewives behind me singing in chorus 'The Grand Old Duke Of York'. I join in and so does Rosie, her mouth bubbling:

> *The Grand Old Duke of York,*
> *He had ten thousand men,*
> *He marched them up to the top of the hill,*
> *And he marched them down again.*
>
> *When they were up they were up,*
> *And when they were down they were down,*

And when they were only half way up
They were neither up nor down.

Another real dark winter's day, Rosie and I are wheeling around the zoo. Except for two couples with buggies, one lone, middle-aged, white Englishman and one lone, young, black man, we have the whole zoo to ourselves. From cage to cage, from garden to garden, we zip. Rosie like me gazes up in awe at the swollen pink bottoms of black monkeys. The notice says that the swollen pink bottoms indicate females in heat. What do you make of that, Rosie? Rosie likes best the giraffes; and so do I. If only all humans were like giraffes – opines our Rosie, methinks. And in the Reptile House we stare at the Nile Alligator and the notice says how the baby in its egg has to cry for its ma to come and hatch it and sometimes the da helps the ma to crack open the egg. Imagine! O I could talk to you, Rosie Joyce, for ever and ever and you are eight months and ten days old today!

And do you know something, Rosie, the last time I was here in Dublin Zoo was with your mother Sarah in 1982, exactly twenty years ago. She was thirteen and she was visiting from Cork. And now here I am brought back again by you, Rosie, her daughter. Twenty years ago. Not exactly twenty *golden* years ago, but not far off that impossible gold. O the gift of life. How fortunate I have been, in spite of everything.

And another thing, Rosie. My own first visit to the zoo was with my mother, Sheila, in 1949 and at the elephant house, which is still the elephant house today, the name of the elephant was Sarah and I had my very first elephant ride on Sarah. How's that! Howdah and all!

And who was the keeper of Sarah the Elephant in Dublin Zoo in 1949? The father of the presenter of this radio programme: Pat Kenny's father!

Tomorrow I hope to visit my mother, Sheila – your great-grandmother, Rosie – and she will say 'It's good to see you' and 'hallo' but maybe not 'goodbye'. Yes, Rosie, a human being is a river, not a rock. I love flowing, don't you? I love everything passing. Death is not death. O Rosie – Rosie Joyce.

March 6, 2002

SEÁN MACBRIDE MEMORIAL MASS

In September 1998 I flew to Japan at the invitation of Professor Masazumi Toraiwa of Waseda University in Tokyo. He struck a generous deal whereby in exchange for my giving poetry readings in Tokyo I would visit Hiroshima. For I am a war baby, born 1944, and, therefore, I grew up in the shadow of Hiroshima: the holocaust of August 6, 1945 when at 8.15 a.m. the Americans dropped the first atomic bomb on the city of Hiroshima, incinerating instantly one hundred thousand innocent men, women and children. Down the years I have read and re-read John Hersey's brief chronicle of that day, a piece of writing as important as the Bible, the Koran and the Talmud all put together.

The other Sunday morning, attending the Seán MacBride Memorial Mass in St Kevin's Oratory – that lovely, classical chapel in Thomas Lane at the rear of the Pro-Cathedral in Dublin, with its golden mosaic of old Kevin – as I sat listening to Captain Jim Kelly chronicling Seán MacBride's life, I called to mind the morning I took the train, the *nozomi* bullet train, to Hiroshima and that afternoon in the Holocaust Museum when I looked at the list of visiting foreign statesman and the only Irish name I could find was the name of Seán MacBride.

My eyes seeped tears: tears of gratitude, tears of anger. It is fashionable nowadays in self-righteous, politically correct, liberal Dublin to scorn the name of Seán MacBride but I, not only as a citizen of Ireland but also as his cousin and godson, felt proud to see his name there and his photograph in the Holocaust Museum in Hiroshima.

The Memorial Mass recalled and celebrated the different facets and periods of Seán MacBride's life. Organised by Ernie Keaveney on behalf of The 1916–1921 Club Incorporating The Old Dublin Brigade IRA, it represented first the republican ancestry and youth of Seán MacBride. For he was the only son of Major John MacBride – my own mother Sheila MacBride's uncle – and of Maud Gonne, my own grand-aunt.

As Captain Kelly reminded us, Seán MacBride, former IRA Chief of Staff, put away the gun for ever in 1937 and became a one hundred per cent constitutional republican and, for the remaining fifty years of his life, worked for human rights here and the world over, on behalf of every class and creed but, most of all, on behalf, in Captain Kelly's phrase, 'of the downtrodden'.

In 1961 in London, along with the English lawyer Peter Bennenson, he founded Amnesty International and became its executive chairman for thirteen years and in 1963 Secretary-General of the International Commission of Jurists in Geneva and, after that, United Nations Commissioner in Namibia. Today in Windhoek, the capital of Namibia, there is a street named after him: *Seán MacBride Avenue*. In 1974 he was awarded the Nobel Peace prize and in 1978 the Lenin Peace prize. At the time I well remember how self-righteous liberals in Dublin accused MacBride of being a Soviet fellow-traveller. The truth, as Captain Kelly quietly recollected, was that in being awarded both the Nobel and Lenin Peace prizes Seán MacBride was a forerunner by twenty years of the *rapprochement* of East and West and of the ending of the Cold War. Seán MacBride was a kind of Gorbachev twenty years before Gorbachev was ever heard of outside the Iron Curtain.

The celebrant of the Memorial Mass was Fr Pat O'Donoghue C.C. who has worked in the Pro-Cathedral for seventeen years. The liturgy was beautiful, simple and moving as was Fr O'Donoghue's homily in which he looked at the word 'intellect' and how Seán MacBride exemplified the hands-on intellectual. Fr O'Donoghue contrasted this image with current attitudes to the so-called mentally handicapped, whose intellects should be esteemed as equally and as admiringly as we esteemed the intellect of Seán MacBride.

Fr O'Donoghue spoke of the unbelievable selfishness of modern society: how we treat the so-called mentally handicapped as second-class citizens and, likewise, the homeless, only worse; especially the alcoholic homeless who die of cold on the streets, sometimes in the doorways of shut churches.

At the end of mass, Fr O'Donoghue gave and sang a beautiful blessing composed by Máire Ní Ghuibhir, formerly of West Cork and now of New Inn, Ballinasloe:

> *Coimirce an athair oraibh*
> *Gach lá agus gach oíche:*
> *Go Dé sibh slán*
> *Faoí Shíochán Chríost*
> *Gach lá agus gach oíche.*

Throughout the Mass, that invigorating mezzo Áiní Ní Channa gave passionate renditions of 'There is a Place', the Alleluia and the Responsorial Psalm 'The Good Man is a Light in the Darkness for the Upright'.

At the back of the oratory, throughout the liturgy, little

Roisín Síle Ní Mhurchú, aged nearly two years and sporting the Mayo colours of red and green, tumbled and danced, danced and tumbled to the edification and merriment of us all. With Jenny Costello on keyboard and Caitriona Lawlor on violin.

After Mass there were to be light refreshments in Wynn's Hotel in Middle Abbey Street. Outside the Pro-Cathedral, the white-haired man in the black leather jacket who'd been standing in front of me at mass asked me in Irish which way to turn. I pointed down Marlborough Street saying 'first turn on the right', so he set off with three women in tow. I'd forgotten about the couple of side-streets in between, so I had to keep shouting from behind 'No, no – it's the next turn to the right.' When I myself reached the corner of Middle Abbey Street, I found the man staring over at Wynn's Hotel in total bafflement. I waved frantically up at the stained-glass sign proclaiming 'Wynn's Hotel'. 'But where is mass?' the man cried. 'We are going to mass!'

'Oh, my God!' I said. 'Were you not the man standing in front of me at Seán MacBride's Memorial Mass?' No, he was not! He was an innocent Irish-speaking Englishman on holiday with his family who happened to be standing at the corner of the Pro-Cathedral searching for the entrance when he had the misfortune to bump into me.

In Wynn's Hotel there was coffee, tea and biscuits. I had the pleasure of meeting some of the old brigade; most especially, an eighty-year-old Dubliner called 'The Strangler Dempsey'. The Strangler used work for the Corporation and whenever he'd spot a dangerous building, he'd say 'We'll strangle that one!'

There was only one thing that puzzled me about the Seán MacBride Memorial Mass, and that was the conspicuous absence of Sinn Féin-IRA. How ironic that, on top of their new respectability, Sinn Féin supported the American policy in Afghanistan of bombing that country into unconditional surrender and the setting up of an illegal concentration camp called 'Camp X-Ray' in Cuba: the kind of abuses of human rights that Seán MacBride had struggled against for most of his life. When it came to the downtrodden people of Afghanistan, where were Caoimhghín Ó Caoláin and Martin Ferris?

I tumbled out of Wynn's Hotel into sunlight and rain, my body full of the words of Isaiah from the first reading at the Memorial Mass for Seán MacBride:

> *Share your bread with the hungry,*
> *and shelter the homeless poor,*
> *clothe the man you see to be naked*
> *and turn not from your own kin ...*
> *If you do away with the yoke,*
> *the clenched fist, the wicked word ...*
> *Your integrity will go before you.*

March 13, 2002

GROUND ZERO

Last Thursday week, March 7, I flew over to New York City for a week for the publication of my new book, *Cries of an Irish Caveman*, and to give two recitals, one at Princeton University in New Jersey and the second at the State Writers Institute in Albany, the state capital of New York.

The publishers have sent a black stretch limo. Staring into the face of the chauffeur, a middle-aged man with a wig of young man's hair, I pretend not to be aware of my dirty shoes and my torn elbows. I jump into the back of the mile-long car and, as to the manner born, stretch my legs in the stretch limo. On the ride into town from JFK I behold how every second house is flying the Stars and Stripes. As the Manhattan skyline drifts up into view, I am aware of the guilt of original sin seeping into my soul. For the rest of the week that seepage will ebb and flow. As we slide into my hotel, the Warwick (War-wick) on West Fifty-fourth Street and Sixth Avenue, a real New York hotel with old-fashioned style, I look at my watch and find that it has stopped. I shake it, slap it, bang it to no avail.

First thing next morning – a warm, sunny morning – I lope around to the nearest Duane Reads, the drugstore chain that stocks everything. I select a $19 watch from the locked showcase. Sharon, a big, cool black woman behind the counter throws a bunch of keys to Sammy, a little Hispanic man, and he unlocks the case. When I've paid Sharon, she drawls out loud and clear 'Give me back the keys, Sammy.'

I walk the blocks. The St Patrick's Day window of Barnes & Noble bookstore at West Forty-eight and Fifth is stacked with *Danny Boy* by Malachy McCourt. On West Fifty-seventh I stumble on Niketown. Bursting through the doors I am confronted by a stocky, bearded, young black man. I say: 'I'm looking for shoes like these,' pointing down at my soiled Nike Max Air Trainers. He says, or I think he says, 'Beautiful Shoes.' 'Oh, yes,' I say. 'Whadya mean?' he says. What he'd actually said was 'Third floor, sir.'

It's twelve noon and the car for Princeton is due at one. I take a snack in a self-service called Mangia on Fifty-seventh and Sixth. At the next table sits the perfect couple, straight out of *The New Yorker* magazine – I mean out of an ad, not out of a cartoon. They are young, in their late twenties. He is tall and broad, short curly black hair and a tanned face; blue, buttoned-down shirt with red arabesque tie and, slung over a chair, a long, navy-blue, lambswool overcoat. She is slender and tall with shoulder-length hair, pendant green ear-rings and perfect white teeth with a hint of buckiness. She is sitting straight up in a lime-green top with a v-neck at the back, skin-tight blue jeans and a pair of blue suede, high-heel stiletto shoes whose toecaps soar upward like streamlined aircraft. The slinkiest shoes I've ever set eyes on and, I bet, not a cent short of a thousand dollars.

The drive out to Princeton, New Jersey takes two hours. The streets of New York are flying banners of defiance. 'New York City & Co. Do your part. Fight back NY. EAT OUT.' 'New York City & Co. Fight back NY. SPEND MONEY.'

'New York City & Co. SALUTE OUR HEROES.' 'New York City & Co. PAINT THE TOWN RED, WHITE AND BLUE.'

My driver is Mr José Andino from Honduras. 'Ground Zero', he tells me, 'is number one tourist attraction right now. Me, I don't want to remember that day. I was driving Tenth and Ninth to collect a lady in Wall St. My wife works two blocks from the World Trade Center. I didn't find my wife until the next day. O God!' He has two daughters, Laura (eleven) and Ellie (six). They are bilingual. They are not allowed to watch TV except animation and Discovery programmes. Gripping the wheel in his white gloves he calls back to me 'I have rules in my house – not like other fathers. My daughters love to read books.'

In my room at the Nassau Inn in Princeton there is a discreet notice on the back of the closet door: 'An iron and ironing board have been provided for your convenience. If you would like to take the iron with you, a charge of $35.00 will be added to your account upon departure.' So much for pinching the iron, which is a cute little Black & Decker Quick 'n' Easy 420 Auto Off.

I spend the next day in MoMA on West Fifty-third at the Retrospective Exhibition of Gerhard Richter, painter, born 1932, Dresden. The most finely curated retrospective I have ever attended, I am flabbergasted by Richter's life's work. I will spend a second day here.

Next morning, Sunday 10, most of the local eateries are shut. On West Fifty-seventh I size up a joint called Wolf's. As I head in the door, I glimpse too late a notice in the window: 'Let Wolf's Cater your SEDER.' I find myself in a crowded Jewish deli. A Gentile man with a shoulder bag, I explode with paranoia. (The TV and papers are full of stories of suicide bombers with shoulder bags walking into Jewish cafes.) Trembling and sweating, I sit down at a table for five. The manager – a huge, young, stubble-bearded Middle-

Eastern Jew – peremptorily switches me to a table for one. I stand up to unzip my jacket, only to find the zip stuck. Surrounded by Jewish families and sprinting Orthodox waiters, I tug at my zip to no avail. Five minutes later and I'm still tugging and hovering there, like a black angel out of Chagall. I accost the manager. I cry: 'I cannot unzip myself.' Sternly, with alacrity and expertise, he puts his hands on my neck and – zoom! – he unzips me quicker than you'd say Melchizedek. I sink down into my seat, ready to faint. I subside on pancakes and fresh orange juice.

It's 11 a.m. and I decide to go down to the other end of Manhattan to the World Trade Center. I take a No. 6 bus down Seventh Avenue, Times Square, Broadway, all the way to Fulton Street. The aim of all terrorists – from al Qaeda to the IRA – is to stop people going about their ordinary business. Did not and will not happen in New York. Yellow Cabs swerve in and out, up and down, with large advertisements attached to their roofs. 'Take me to URINETOWN – the Musical.'

A middle-aged man asks the bus driver 'What do I do at Ground Zero?' The driver – a big, kindly, red-headed black woman says: 'You just look, sir – you'll see.' She cries out: 'Next stop – Ground Zero.' I get a ticket slot for 5.30 p.m. I wander around Greenwich Village and browse in a bookstore called 'Unoppressive Non-Imperialist Bargain Books'. It's next door to a hairdressers called 'Hairhoppers'. I slip into the Scalabrinian Church on Carmine and Bleecker and try to say a prayer or two.

On the walkway up to the viewing platform at the World Trade Center site, I read in blue biro amongst thousands of scribbled messages: 'I believe there is no "us" and "them" only us – all of us "little humans".' On the platform, gazing into the pits of hell, I chat with a short, blonde, blue-eyed policewoman in plainclothes. She shrugs her shoulders and asks me: 'So what is it with religion? You're Irish, you should know.' A detective for nineteen years, she hopes to retire this summer.

That night on CBS TV there's a documentary entitled '9/11' made by two young French brothers, Jules and Gideon. Last summer with the help of fireman James Hanlon they started making a documentary about a young rookie fireman or 'Proby' called Tony Benetato. They film him through the summer as he waits for his first fire. We hear Tony saying: 'I could have been a lawyer but I wanted to do something I could live with. I can live with this.' On the morning of September 11, Tony gets left behind to mind the phones while his comrades race into the first tower. The French brothers get separated. Jules, with a camera, is in the lobby of the first tower. Through his camera we see the catastrophe from inside the tower. It's like underwater filming. We see a fire chief in the smoke and dust swimming around with his torch. I hope to God that RTÉ TV will show this documentary someday soon. Only a humane, truth-telling, disinterested documentary such as this can show you the pure evil of terrorism, be it al Qaeda or IRA.

Other nights I watch Chris Matthews, New York's answer to Vincent Browne. 'I'm Chris Matthews and I'm talking HARDBALL. Why should we go kick butt in Syria? Have we the right to lob something into their country and blow half of it away? Now, let me tell you what I really think. We should get these body-snatchers out of the Pentagon. I'm Chris Matthews and I'm talking HARDBALL.'

On Wednesday at the New York Public Library I attend a discussion called *Beyond the Blarney: Talking About the Irish in America*. Maureen Dezell of the *Boston Globe*, Terry Golway of the *New York Observer*, Emer Martin, Dublin-born novelist living in California, talk sense and wit. But the flame of the evening is Colm Tóibín, whose refrain is 'My father's house has many mansions' and who tells the story of Henry James's father who was a Presbyterian from Cavan and whose

Presbyterian concept of liberty we in Ireland today would do well to heed.

Next morning, Thursday, I take an Amtrak train from Penn Station to Albany; a two and a half hour ride up along the banks of the River Hudson. At Yonkers station a notice says: 'If you're inclined to live on the edge, please do it somewhere other than on this platform.'

Friday I take the same train back and fly out from Newark. In the line for Gateway Security, I watch the Port Authority of NYC Pipe & Drum Band form a circle of portly men in tartan skirts with sporrans dangling from paunches as they play 'The Minstrel Boy' and 'The Wearing of the Green'. I have an aisle seat with, inside me, two young men from Minnesota making their first trip abroad, destination Shannon. Dan Berg and Shawn Olson. Exuberant and excited, they will hire a Nissan Micra and tour Mayo, Galway, Clare, Kerry and Dublin for two weeks. They anoint me with their innocence and I step off at Dublin with Minnesota sunlight in the square of my soul.

March 20, 2002

Home from Italy

After five weeks working in Italy, I find myself back home in Dublin in a 'state' of culture shock. I say 'state': I mean not only my own 'state' but the 'State' we call Ireland. As I scuttle through Dublin airport on the way to baggage retrieval I feel that I am no longer in Europe. Except for the euro coins in my pockets, I have left Europe. I am back in Ireland which is not Europe. This is a sickening feeling. Like carsickness: nausea; dizziness. Lurching at the baggage carousel I feel disorientated, so much so that when my two bags fail to emerge I am not grief-stricken as I usually am when my bags go missing; I am hardly even greatly interested. At most I am irritated. I jump up into the coach for the long-term car-park and try to engage the driver in conversation but he is too bored; affable but bored. I drive into the city and, of course, the first things I see are the General Election posters and these only serve to increase my disorientation and loss. 'Where am I?' I keep muttering to myself at each set of traffic lights. And I keep answering 'You're in Ireland, silly.' But a deeper, calmer, more austere voice keeps whispering: You Are Not in Europe Anymore.

On Easter Monday April 1, I flew from Dublin via Milan to Florence. That was the day that al Qaeda were due to plant bombs at Florence Airport, according to the United States Government who, with their customary egotism and irresponsibility, had broadcast these threats without consulting the Italian Government. We touched down at Florence Airport at 10.20 p.m. where I was due to be met by a Moroccan driver by the name of Mohammed. We had not met before. Nor did I know then what I learned weeks later when Mohammed and I had become good friends: that his instructions were 'Paul Durcan is Irish and he is a poet and he looks very sad.'

Mohammed is a tall, thin, quietly courteous Moroccan man in his mid-thirties from the mountains of the High Atlas who has spent the last seventeen years working in Milan and only recently moved to the vicinity of Florence. He had with him a local Italian man in his sixties, Raphaelo, who, I realised, was acting as navigator. But like many a wise man with local knowledge, Raphaelo knew too much for other people's good and after half an hour it was plain that we were lost, and so a journey that would normally take forty-five minutes took two hours. It was a matter of trying to get off the wrong *autostrada* and link up with the right *autostrada*. At one point, at a spaghetti junction not far off one of the several available *autostrada*, we came upon a roadblock set up by four carloads of gun-holstered *carabinieri*. So this is my fate – I said to myself in the back seat. To be arrested as an al Qaeda suspect on a minor road in Tuscany in the company of a young Moroccan man. The *carabinieri* shone two torches into the battered old white Honda Civic Estate and scrutinised each face. Then a quick fusillade of interrogation. Raphaelo, the local man, whose own father in World War II was the *capo* of the partisans in the area we were trying to locate, had only to say a few words and the *carabinieri* waved us on. Whereupon, Mohammed went to drive in one direction, only to be ordered by Raphaelo to drive in the opposite direction. Raphaelo, for all the world, looked and sounded, every small, slender, silvery millimetre of him, like an understated man from Mayo. As we chugged around in more circles, he murmured to Mohammed 'Il terrorismo.'

We reached our destination, the hilltop village of Donnini, one thousand feet above sea-level, twenty-seven kilometres south-east of Florence, and, about four kilometres beyond it, half-way down a medieval, unpaved track, a medieval farmhouse called Santa Maddalena where I was to spend most of the next five weeks living and working. In the dark we stumbled across a small olive grove to a tower where I would sleep and work. In medieval times the tops of these towers were used to light fires on and send smoke signals from.

The next morning was a sunny day, one of the few in April in Tuscany which was mostly Irish weather, broken and damp. I found that the little farm was perched on the edge of a ravine among many other ravines in the forests of the mountains south-east of Florence. I walked slowly along the edge of the little olive grove the sixty yards to the farmhouse for breakfast, its sandstone walls gleaming in purple wisteria and yellow roses. I walked under small ancient oaks and a walnut; past a thirty-foot-high bamboo grove; and finally under an ancient mulberry. At the big gate the biggest and reddest peony I have ever seen. Through the weeks I watched the death of The Great Peony. Along all the skylines, lines of black cypresses.

At the table of the household the predominant language was, naturally, Italian, followed by French. Occasionally, out of courtesy to me, English. And Arabic and Albanian. Meals were leisurely and intense and hilarious. The main topic was always Israel-Palestine and while there was not one iota of anti-Semitism in the conversation – indeed most of the speakers came from families who had suffered at the hands of the Nazis – anger with Israel and with the bull Sharon was superseded only by anger with President Bush and the current US administration which seems so ardent on leading us all into World War III. National politics was treated with exasperated incredulity, Berlusconi being regarded as a stage-Italian, a fake Roman Emperor.

Very quickly, Ireland seemed to be not just fifteen hundred terrestrial kilometres away but spiritually thousands of miles away. Very quickly, Ireland was a hard place to imagine; a dark island somewhere east of Iceland, west of Norway. Very quickly, I realised I was at the heart of Europe and that the heart of Europe is orientated Eastwards, not Westwards. (Twenty years ago in Paris I could hear the same message but failed to listen to it.) The hinterlands of the minds of we Irish are the UK on the one hand and the USA on the other hand. But the hinterlands of people's minds here in Italy are Turkey, Armenia, Palestine, Israel, Romania, Egypt, Syria, Iraq, Iran, Tunisia, Morocco, Afghanistan. From the smallest details of life to the largest, we were always facing East. For the other people at the table, cities and provinces like Mazar-e-Sharif or the Bukovina or Damascus or Bethlehem or Amman or Tunis or Addis Ababa were places they had all visited and knew well. And so for me the Semitic and Arab and Asian worlds ceased to be the caricatures of the English-language western media and became real places with real, identifiable people who have little in common with the West except their humanity.

At table I heard stories about certain American and Israeli politicians which would make the protagonists of the Irish tribunals look like fairies – good fairies.

Conversation was always courteous, no matter what the content. For example, when the topic of the business and personal connections between the Bush and Bin Laden families was under discussion, everybody spoke quietly, even sadly.

Courtesy: that was something that struck me again and again at mealtimes in Santa Maddalena. In the space of five weeks in that Tuscan household, I came to feel that good manners are more important than any ideology.

I felt homesick for Ireland and yet increasingly angry with my native land. Realising how for thirty years we have milked Europe of money and yet we have refused to take on any European values ourselves. Except for six or seven little towns, like Westport, Co. Mayo or Enniscorthy, Co. Wexford, our lifestyle remains as non-European as it was before we joined the European Union. We have refused the civilising influences of Europe and instead have become a cultural satellite of the USA and the UK

Walking the streets of Florence, Donnini, Arrezo, Pontasieve, Rignano, Pelago, Regello, I felt ashamed to be Irish, ashamed to be a citizen of a country which is so selfish and so self-centred that we rejected the Nice Treaty. Irish selfishness is now an international phenomenon.

Back in Dublin I drive out to the far, pale suburbs to visit my mother enduring Alzheimer's disease. She looks up at me and smiles: 'Have I seen *you* somewhere before?' We sit out in the garden admiring a great cedar. In silence. I struggle with my grief and my anger. The roads of Dublin full of grotesque electioneering posters. When I was the child of my worried young mother in the 1940s and 1950s, the great slogans were 'Health'; 'Education'; 'Transport'. O Mummy! Here we are fifty years later, still with no health service. Still with no transport. Still with no fair and broad education. Still the Haves refusing to share with the Have Nots.

I find a rubber football under a hedge and throw it to Mummy. We play Donkey. After fifteen or sixteen throws I am the first to drop the ball.

From indoors brays the voice of a man the same age as myself: 'Juliet! Juliet! Juliet, Juliet, Juliet, Juliet.'

May 15, 2002

BALLYMAHON

Last Friday morning at 10.30 a.m., in pelting rain and storm-force gales, I set off from Ballymahon, Co. Longford to drive back to Ringsend, Dublin. As I rode along the road from Ballymahon to Mullingar, I felt a burst of gratitude for being still alive at all on Planet Earth at the age of fifty-seven and, in particular, for being alive at the wheel of a car driving along the Ballymahon-Mullingar road, the R392, on a wild wet morning in May.

There is no more sympathetic road in Ireland than the R392: the Ballymahon-Mullingar road. It's about twenty miles. Almost all of it is straight as a die but chopped into steep hills and steep dips. Literally, *up hill and down dale* all the way from Ballymahon to Mullingar.

The sides of the road are lined with thousands upon thousands of souls waving in the wind – the white souls of cow-parsley, four, five, six deep; rows upon rows of cheering cow-parsley jumping up and down in the hedgerows either side of the road. Or Queen Anne's lace, as they call cow-parsley in Meath.

And the white souls also of thousands upon thousands of hawthorn trees in blossom, blossoming baking-powder white over all the meadows and ring forts. Such whiteness in the dark eye of the storm! Only last night, in bed in Ballymahon, I read in a book called *Exchanging Hats* that the poet and painter Elizabeth Bishop considered *white* to be the colour of 'impassioned reassurance'. How about that, then – 'white is the colour of impassioned reassurance'.

The Ballymahon-Mullingar road! The R392! May the planners never widen you, never flatten you, never take the kinks out of your hair – your up-hill and down-dale ankle-length hair.

And as I drive along, I drive at not more than 35 m.p.h. – a lesson Christy Moore in his four-wheel drive taught me nine years ago in the vicinity of Yellow Furze, his mother's home place on the Boyne between Navan and Drogheda. There is scarcely another car or lorry on the road and, having to head back to Dublin, I want to savour every half-mile of it. I ride through the villages of Moyvore and Rathconrath. Easy and slow I take the crooked bridge over the Royal Canal. And as I approach the hems of the outskirts of Mullingar, the twin towers of its cathedral kneeling to my left, minding its chapels of mosaics of *St Patrick Lighting the Paschal Fire at Slane* and of *St Anne Presenting the Virgin Mary in the Temple* by the Russian mosaicist Boris Anrep, he who made the mosaic floors of the National Gallery in London (who, I wonder, was the avant-garde bishop or parish priest who commissioned these Mullingar mosaics?), the penny drops. I should say: the one euro drops.

How fortunate I am to be driving along the most beautiful road in Ireland while five or ten thousand miles away on a remote Pacific island named Saipan the men of Ireland are dragging down the name of my nation – all that scapegoating, all that thoughtlessness – and India and Pakistan are playing nuclear hooligans. The coin lying at the bottom of my well of well-being is the coin of having slept the previous night for the very first time in my life under the roof of my daughter. Life, birth and death have come full circle. She, who once was a child under my fleeting roof in Cork, last night in Ballymahon gave a roof to her itinerant father. Never have I slept so soundly, sleeping under my daughter's roof.

Three years ago Síabhra – whose name is a thousands of years old Gaelic Indo-European name meaning 'Virgin Bringer of the Snows' – with her man Blaise Drummond moved into a seemingly uninhabitable, derelict, small one-and-a-half-storey farmhouse dating from around the year 1800 – the Act of Union. No running water. They sunk their own well and now drink the best water in the country. No electricity, no phone. Now there is an I-Mac computer with printer and scanner in the guest bedroom.

From that day three years ago in May 1999 almost to this day, the two of them have lived in the house while at the same time excavating it and restoring it with the steadfast advice of local craftsman Aidan Quinn and wheelbarrows of patience.

It remains an enigma to their friends as well as to their nearest and dearest how they survived living there in those conditions and how they persevered. Such was the dust during most of the three years – but especially during the digging up of the foundations – that even one single, overnight item of clothing had to be covered if it was to survive. All I know is that every Saturday night they used tune in to Philip King's wireless programme from Ballyferriter, *South Wind Blows*.

But dig up the foundations they did, Blaise breaking his back in the process. Kango hammer, shovel, pickaxe. Dug down deep to bedrock and laid down heating pipes before laying a floor of sandstone flags transported all the way from the quarry in Lacken, Co. Mayo. Lacken flags.

They re-roofed the house, inside and out, restoring the original tongue-and-groove ceilings.

Three years later the house remains to have the finishing touches put to its interior but to me it is the equal of a small house in St Petersburg, a Pushkin dream-cabin on the shores of the Neva. (For Neva read Shannon: the house stands in the corner of a field between the Inny and the Tang rivers as they converge to enter the River Shannon.) All its walls and all its ceilings are painted white and furnished with Mediterranean warmth and Japanese simplicity. It is a quietly warm house of four white rooms and a bathroom which architectural historians, I bet, will be queuing up to visit in the years to come. Already, the German art publishing house Taschen have published a photograph of its restored Raeburn stove in the recently published *Country Kitchens and Recipes* (2001).

Last night as I lay down under the white duvet in the white guestroom of my daughter's home, I felt the peace of her blessing but also the peace of that which is very old by virtue of being loved adequately enough to be made new and whole again. I felt the peace of all that is contrary to the callous egotism of ribbon development. This ancient, two-hundred-year-old, humble farmhouse with its three-foot-thick walls and its deep window sills has been restored with love; love that is not ephemeral infatuation but love that is patient and faithful and prepared to endure the onslaughts of time and the weather. Love that is a marriage with life.

And yet, I realise I have fundamentally misrepresented the restoration. For the farmhouse stands in a garden of one acre and I realise that Síabhra and Blaise see the garden around the house as being as much part of the architecture as the walls and the roof. I realise that these two young people see house and garden as indivisible. So the young tree planted on a small hill of earth in the south-west corner of the acre is as

PAUL DURCAN'S *diary*

much part of the architecture as the new wooden staircase in the house. It is an *Ailanthus altissima* or 'Tree of Heaven'. In the south-east corner on a hillock is a mature sycamore, protective, swaying in the wind like a ship's doctor. In the north-west corner is a beech tree which must be at least two hundred years old, the same age as the house. My God, in that year of our Lord 1800, the Act of Union, the man and woman of this house must have planted that beech! On the north-east terrace only two weeks ago Síabhra laid down retained-by-planks beds of lettuces, spinaches, carrots, potatoes. On the south terrace a flowerbed newly dug by Blaise: pink pokers, hostas, ferns.

And so to bed in Ringsend, Dublin. I take down from the shelves two books by Josef Pieper whose titles speak not only for themselves but for all of us ordinary, refusing-to-Saipan folk in Ireland, Japan, Pakistan, India and, most especially, Síabhra and Blaise in Ballymahon: *In Tune with the World: a theory of festivity* published 1965 and *Leisure is the Basis of Culture*, 1952.

And as in Ringsend, Dublin I doze into blotched, solo sleep, the coincidence occurs to me that Ballymahon is the home place of the itinerant poet Oliver Goldsmith. Sweet Auburn! Goldsmithstown! The Deserted Village no longer Deserted! Lost vagabond, whose soul has been restored to his tough, idyllic hearth.

May 29, 2002

LETTER TO CARDINAL CONNELL

My dear Desmond, Cardinal Archbishop of Dublin,

How are you on this November winter's morning? How are you doing? Did you say mass at an early hour in your private chapel? At 7 a.m. alone or with members of your palace household in Drumcondra by the Tolka?

When I was a boy of eleven years I used love cycling the empty Dublin streets in the pre-dawn darkness to serve 7 a.m. mass in one of the tiny oratories at my Jesuit school in Ranelagh. There would be just the priest and myself in an oratory so tiny there was scarcely any space for the server. It was like saying mass in a secret cupboard in penal times. I loved serving mass. The different priests had their different ways of doing the same thing and I cherished each priest's idiosyncrasy. One man would intone at a million miles per hour; another man would intone as slowly as a wheelbarrow. I loved handling the cruets of wine and water. I loved ringing the bells at the sanctus and the consecration and the communion. I loved watching the priest donning his vestments. Putting on the surplice over his rumpled shirt and worn baggy trousers. The alb of the liturgical day – green or red or violet or white. I loved the mixture of aromas. Of the red altar wine and the Eucharistic wafers and of the musty carpet and of human night sweat. I loved the Latin responses: *Introibo ad altare Dei; Ad Deum qui laetificat juventutem meam.* I loved cycling back to my mother's kitchen in time for porridge and the sponsored programmes on Radio Éireann. Irish Christianity was the mother tongue of my soul and it remains the mother tongue of my soul in spite of the institution of the Irish Roman Catholic Church.

When you said mass this morning did you say it in Latin or in English or in Irish? I try to imagine what it must be like for you in these terrible times to say mass in spite of all the public criticism that has been heaped on you. I see hovering over your head not the Paraclete, not the white dove of the Holy Spirit but the big black logo of the calamitous phrase 'CHILD ABUSE'. I see and hear your spiritual concentration being broken into and entered at every turn of the mass and at every bend of the road of prayer. At the very moment of the consecration, the big black phrase 'CHILD ABUSE' runs rings around your soul like a rat on a roulette table. As you disrobe in the sacristy, I see lumps of a desolate melancholy flaking off you like bits of crust off a stale loaf.

But it is not about 'CHILD ABUSE' that I am writing to you. In fact, of course, the phrase 'child abuse' is itself an abuse of language. The outrage is about child rape and child buggery and child terror, not child abuse. I am writing to you simply as a parishioner of the Archdiocese of Dublin who feels that, apart from your problems with supervising and tending the sick and troubled members of your clergy, you have not, down these fourteen years of your ministry, been a shepherd to your flock in any believable or rudimentary sense of the word shepherd. What were your feelings, I wonder, last Sunday at mass when you heard the first reading from

Malachi 1: 14 – 'You have strayed from the way; you have caused many to stumble by your teaching.'

Three years ago RTÉ Radio 1 broadcast a series entitled *A Giant at my Shoulder*. Contributors were invited to talk for thirty minutes about the person who had most influenced their lives. I found myself in the dilemma of being forced to choose between Mohammed Ali, formerly Cassius Clay, and John XXIII, formerly Angelo Roncalli. For both of these wonderful shepherds, human existence posed one fundamental problem: the existential problem of how to practise affection on a minute-to-minute basis, day in, day out. Can it be done?

I chose to talk about John XXIII and I began my broadcast by recalling that Tuesday night October 28, 1958 when, sitting on my mother's bed listening to the wireless, I heard the Radio Éireann commentator in Rome observe white smoke and an hour later an aged voice crying from the balcony of St Peter's: *Annunciamamus gaudium magnum ... Habemus Papam ... Eminentissimum, Reverendissimum dominum – dominum Angelum Giuseppum Sante Romani Ecclesiae Cardinale RONCALLI!*

For the next five years, even though I was a young Dubliner living under the Kremlin-like rule of Archbishop McQuaid, I watched in amazement and delight as John XXIII with his mother-hen personality went about practising his message of affection and being a shepherd not only to his own flock but to all mankind. Last Sunday's Letter from Paul to the Thessalonians was the voice of John XXIII: 'Like a mother feeding and looking after her own children, we felt so devoted and protective towards you ...'

In the early 1960s I was a student in UCD and I remember the sunlight and the breezes emanating from Pope John's eyes and from his feet and from his lips. At that time, dear Desmond, Cardinal Archbishop, you were a lecturer in the Department of Philosophy in UCD. My impression of you as a philosopher was that you were hostile to the modern world, especially to the great modern philosophies and theologies of existentialism as represented by Sartre, Heidegger, Camus, Marcel, Küng, Schillebeeckx, Baum, Boff and John XXIII himself.

Since your elevation to Dublin in 1988, you have helped to empty not only the archdiocese of Dublin but also the whole island of Ireland of the maternal spirit of John XXIII. Instead, for fourteen years you have filled my soul with fear, despondency and loneliness. Watching you looming on the altar of the Pro-Cathedral, or in a sermon droning, I feel as if I am in an airbus at thirty-six thousand feet in the vicinity of the North Pole. Your countenance and your vocabulary constitute snow-white desolation, vast empty tundra, eternally wailing emptiness.

Today is the Feast of Leonard, patron saint of prisoners. In your celebration of mass this morning, did you pray for all of the thousands upon thousands of Irish Christians who are prisoners of Irish church history? In the fourteen years of your ministry, I do not recall one single affectionate gesture or homily or letter or pronouncement. All I recall is complaint. Of President McAleese for taking communion in the Church of Ireland. Of Bishop Walton Empey for not being a 'high-flying' theologian. Of Trinity College Dublin for not recognising you in the correct way. Of homosexual people for being homosexual. Of Bishop Casey for being heterosexual in the wrong way. Your peculiar attitudes to female sexuality and celibacy. (By the way, is it true that you have opposed the return to Ireland of the tragic Eamonn Casey? If it be true, I must tell you that I do not comprehend such mercilessness not only towards Eamonn Casey himself but towards the people of Galway. In the 1990s you enabled Ireland to become not only the Celtic Tiger but also a merciless society.)

As the Responsorial Psalm had it last Sunday: 'A weaned child on its mother's breast, even so is my soul.'

My dear Desmond, Cardinal Archbishop of Dublin, I hope you are doing all right this morning in spite of everything.

Glory to God in the highest, and on earth peace to men of goodwill.

Yours sincerely,
Paul Durcan

November 6, 2002

THE FIRST CHILD PSYCHIATRIST
OF THE WESTERN WORLD

The odd visitor to my cave in Ringsend has been known to raise an eyebrow at the exhibition inside my hall door of a framed facsimile of the 1916 Proclamation. No apologies. The IRA Sinn Féin Thirty Years War of terror does not nullify the values proclaimed by Patrick Pearse in 1916. Of all the aspirations in the Proclamation, the Republic's guarantee 'to cherish all the children of the nation equally' is the aspiration that most sings to me and so on Friday, November 1, the Feast of All Saints, I attended a symposium in Galway on Child and Adolescent Psychiatry. The occasion was the retirement of Dr Anthony Carroll, first Clinical Director of Child and Adolescent Psychiatry in the Western Health Board, 1975–2002. On Dr Carroll's appointment in 1975 there was a staff of one: himself. Now he departs leaving a staff of ninety in the child psychiatric service in the West.

It was a strange and memorable day: strange because of the shameful statistics for the rest of Ireland outside the West; memorable because of the obvious need and desire of all the medical participants to celebrate the pioneering work and extraordinary career of Dr Carroll.

The first talk by Dr Colette Halpin, Consultant Child Psychiatrist, Portlaoise General Hospital, gave us a history of child and adolescent psychiatry in Ireland. With the exception of voluntary inpatient services set up by the St John of God Brothers in Dublin in 1951 (now closed down) and the purpose-built unit set up by the voluntary service of the Brothers of Charity in Mahon in Cork, from 1922 to 1968 there was no public health child and adolescent psychiatric service in Ireland. Whatever *were* the priorities of the new Irish state 1922–1968 – all of forty-six years – the mental health of children and adolescents was not one of them.

In 1968 the Eastern Health Board created the first post in Ireland of a Clinical Director of Child Psychiatry, Dr Paul McCarthy, catering for Dublin, Kildare and Wicklow.

Seven years later, in 1975, thanks to the commitment of its Chief Executive Officer Eamonn Hannon, the Western Health Board appointed their first Clinical Director of Child Psychiatry, Dr Carroll. Three years later, in 1978, the Midland Health Board followed suit. But the Southern Health Board did not appoint a child psychiatrist until 1994. Cork took all of seventy years to get around to appointing a child psychiatrist.

So the story is that, in the eighty-year lifespan of the Irish State, children's mental health has not been cherished except by a small band of volunteer Brothers of religious orders and of dedicated pioneers such as Dr Anthony Carroll. And, in so far as children are cherished today, there is, said Dr Colette Halpin, 'a total lack of equity in terms of access to services'.

In the Ireland of my generation – I was born in 1944 – women were regarded by churchmen and politicians as a necessary irrelevance; but irrelevant as women were, children were more irrelevant. State and Church camouflaged their neglect by the Madonna-and-child strategy of paying lip service to women and children: that is, of idealising women and children.

Dr Halpin concluded by showing how, while in recent years there has been a slight improvement in *outpatient* facilities for children and adolescents in need of psychiatric care, *inpatient* services are 'in a state of total crisis'. There are only three *inpatient* facilities in the Republic of Ireland: St Anne's Children's Centre in Galway, founded by Dr Carroll in 1979, which has approximately twelve beds, Warrenstown House and Court Hall in Dublin.

Our child and adolescent psychiatric service in Ireland is unbelievably understaffed. In the health service today, there are forty-five child and adolescent psychiatrists. Forty-five! Can you believe it? And wait for it: we have ten psychiatrists for children with learning problems and disabilities. Dr Halpin estimated that for Ireland to have even a minimally adequate service we would need 120 child psychiatrists.

Dr Kate Ganter of the Lucena Clinic in Dublin looked at Dr Halpin's scenario in more detail. 'At the best of times,' she reported, 'children are forgotten and, at the worst of times, they are not seen.'

Dr Richard Williams, Professor of Mental Health Services at the University of Glamorgan, gave us an eagle's eye view of services in Wales and in England, where the situation is almost as dire as it is in Ireland – 'adult-focused instead of being, as it should be, child-centred'. He described child psychiatrists as 'heroes working in a vacuum'. He singled out Dr Carroll as being a hero of our time.

The final two speakers were Karin Grieve, social worker and psychotherapist at Lyradoon Family Centre in Salthill opened by Dr Carroll in 1976, and Clare Gormley, senior psychologist and family therapist also at Lyradoon. Each described what an inspiring leader Dr Carroll had been. The picture was of a child psychiatrist for whom creativity and playfulness are the key to health. The good child psychiatrist is the one who, first of all, unlocks his or her own individual creativity and playfulness and, secondly, the creativity and playfulness of the child and/or adolescent. The kernel of childhood and adolescence – and especially of all childhood and adolescent therapy – is creativity and playfulness. Dr Carroll has a passion for the mysterious, sacramental efficacies of language, art, play, symbolism, storytelling and affection. As a physician there was nothing in all the minutiae of life that was not grist to his mill. 'The Wizard' – the beloved Dr Carroll has been called.

Commemorated also was the Inishbofin Seminar in the 1970s when, in the company of Dr Carroll, Mary Banotti put Irish child psychiatry through her ecstatic hoops. Clare Gormley spoke of Inishbofin and post-Inishbofin. She also emphasised Dr Carroll's educational commitment to child psychiatry and his vocational training of Senior Registrars. She paid tribute to what she termed Dr Carroll's 'collegiate' style of leadership and of his loyalty to his staff and his courage in facing up to external pressure. She described the huge importance Dr Carroll attached to keeping the rituals of seasonal festivals such as Christmas in the children's centres which he had founded. Karin Grieve told how at one Christmas party Santa's present for Dr Carroll was a cap with two peaks which bore the legend: 'I am their leader – which way did they go?'

Finally, reluctantly (he is a man of notorious modesty), Dr Carroll stepped up to the microphone to say that he was not going to speak but, in a characteristic throwaway, he acknowledged that 'it is terribly stressful working in a vacuum'. As I glanced at this unassuming, convivial, thorny, sparkling man, I saw thirty-five years of winter afternoons and his warming the embers of each child's creativity, warming them to a blaze. On the question of how and why thirty-five years ago he became a child psychiatrist he said: 'When I was fourteen my father said to me: "You've got the wrists of a jockey." I said to my father: "That's interesting because I think I have the wrists of a child psychiatrist."' He chuckled his famous uninhibited chuckle and he was gone – the first child psychiatrist of the western world.

November 13, 2002

LETTER TO GERRY ADAMS

Dear Gerry Adams,

That photograph of you three Wednesdays ago with the six-month-old baby boy perched inside the Sam Maguire Cup at Stormont: what a stunning photograph! And on the front page of *The Irish Times*, and at the top of the front page! A photograph of the year! Choc-a-bloc with innocence and fun and in the background the baby's mother, Sinn Féin MP Michelle Gildernew, laughing proudly with delight. I could not deny all that innocent fun any more than I could deny your own enjoyment of the spectacle of the baby boy crawling in the cradle of the Sam Maguire cup on a mahogany table in the halls of Stormont Castle, October 29, 2002. And who was the photographer? Paul Faith/P.A!

Yet also I felt despair. For what the photograph was proclaiming was the final and total victory of your Thirty Years War. I realised again the truth of the First Article in the Handbook of Political and Military Terror: that Time is always on the side of the victor. I use the word 'terror' scrupulously and not as a term of abuse. When the IRA went into action in the early 1970s it used terror as a textbook strategy to defeat not only the British Army and the RUC but to defeat every citizen who stood in the IRA's way. It used terror knowing that terror's greatest ally is the Process of Time itself, how the Process of Time is a process of Attrition and Oblivion so that we ordinary folk have no choice but to accept the end result of terror, primarily because we cannot remember the day-by-day, hour-by-hour minutiae of terror. It's hard enough to recall the minutiae and shape of the last three weeks; it is impossible to recall the shape and texture, the three-hundred-thousand contexts, the three-hundred-thousand sub-contexts of the three hundred thousand hours of the last thirty years.

I was twenty-six in 1970 so I have been around for every murder and massacre, whereas the succeeding generations who are reaping the harvest of your war have little or no memory of what you did.

The horrors of the 1970s, 1980s and 1990s! Bloody Sunday – a massacre perpetrated by a notoriously stupid regiment of the British Army. Followed by IRA murders day after day after day, year after year after year of innocent people. On a September morning in 1974 the Belfast IRA murdered two judges at their breakfasts.

This marvellous photograph of you as a smiling, benign, handsome, gentle godfather of the six-month-old baby boy in the Sam Maguire Cup at Stormont fills me with such despair that my eyes leak tears; tears of anguish that you did what you did and that you have been rewarded with victory. I have no choice but to accept your victory but I cannot forgive you for what you did.

In the 1970s I was living in Cork, but normal, decent, humane family life was impossible. Every evening on the TV news the latest footage of IRA killing. One evening in 1976 the 6 p.m. footage was of a pool of blood in Newry and the newscaster saying 'Today a Protestant man was shot dead in Newry.' My six-year-old daughter Sarah playing on the floor with her crayons looked up at me and asked: 'What is a Protestant, Daddy?'

I cannot forgive you. It's not a matter of intellectual choice. I *cannot* forgive you. You had lawful ideals but not one of those ideals could justify even one of the hundreds and hundreds of murders and massacres.

Take even just that one murder in Newry in 1976. Do you remember the man's name? Let us cradle that man's skull in the Sam Maguire Cup on the mahogany table and, holding it up to the TV camera, let us contemplate the brain cells of his skull, the beautifully intricate structures of his grey matter, the circuitry of his prefrontal cortex, the plasticine of his frontal lobes.

Your endurance and your skill are beyond question. But I cannot accept the Thirty Years War – not only the killing of people but also the killing of language, the abuse, manipulation, murder of words. My soul is coated with the excrement of thirty years of propaganda. And in your voice those terrifying notes of intimidation and self-pity: 'I am here to progress the peace process, not to react to the stories of some jumped-up, scurrilous journalist.'

The baby in the cup, six-month-old Emmet Gildernew, when he is eighteen I reckon that Sinn Féin IRA will be the leading party in both governments in Ireland and that all your TDs and MLAs will have injected the new generations with your official mythology of the Thirty Years War and you yourself will be in your early seventies and you will be ensconced in Áras an Uachtaráin as President of the Republic of Ireland and all the people will be saying as you jet around the globe – 'Isn't President Adams the best president we've ever had? Better even than Mary McAleese and Mary Robinson.'

Oh, but in the killing estates of Time that photograph of

the baby in the cup stalks me. Obviously some kind of senior editorial decision was taken in *The Irish Times* to install at the top of the front page this amazing graphic of sentimentality, this homage to Gerry Adams as the Father Christmas not just of 2002 but of the last thirty years: Gerry Adams as the Santa Claus of Irish History; Father of all that has been, is and is to come.

What was the thinking behind the editorial decision to publish this portrait of President Gerry Adams as the Queen Victoria of modern Irish history, smiling dotingly at his little Lord Fauntleroy popping up out of the silverware? Did the new editor give her editorial blessing to this sensational development in Irish journalism? What part did the brilliant Sinn Féin propaganda unit play in staging the photograph?

As I stare at the photograph and reread the caption, I realise for the first time that the caption actually suggests that it was you yourself, Gerry Adams, who engineered the whole thing. The caption reads: 'Sinn Féin president Mr Gerry Adams lifts six-month-old Emmet Taggert Gildernew, son of Sinn Féin MP for Fermanagh South Tyrone, Ms Michelle Gildernew (left) into the Sam Maguire trophy at a reception at Stormont ...' So it was you yourself who thought of lifting the little baby boy into the cup.

The stomach of my soul seizes up and I wonder if the neighbours can hear me as I retch on the floor of the morgue. All these hundreds and hundreds and hundreds of unique individual human beings murdered, many of them much more interesting and decent people than you or I, Gerry Adams, all of them dumped into the trash can of history, their rotting arms and legs hanging out of bins everywhere, on new estates and on seashores and in derelict bogs. And you in your suit and collar and tie putting your dainty fifty-four-year-old forefinger into the tiny hand of a six-month-old baby boy whom you've chosen to plant in the silver cup of the Sam Maguire trophy. No, no, no, no, no. I refuse. I refuse to accept it now or ever. I refuse.

Slán,

Paul Durcan

November 21, 2002

POSTSCRIPT: LETTER TO GERRY ADAMS

Dear Gerry Adams,

Your supporters condemn me because most of my anger has been directed against the IRA and not the loyalists and the British Army. That is true except to say that the many poems I have written out of the Northern Nightmare include poems about the massacre of the Miami Show Band 1975, the Dublin Massacre 1974, a tribute to RTÉ Reporter Liam Hourican 1974 and the murders of the two young friends in Poyntzpass in 1998, Philip Allen and Damian Trainor.

I come from a West of Ireland nationalist republican family. In 1948 my father stood as a Clann na Poblachta candidate in Mayo. My mother's name is Sheila MacBride. In 1916 her father, Joseph MacBride, was imprisoned in Gloucester Jail and after his election to the first Dáil he was taken hostage by the Black and Tans. His younger brother, John MacBride, was executed by the British Army in 1916, on May 5 at 3.47 a.m. John MacBride was my mother's uncle and godfather and his only son, Seán MacBride, was my

135

cousin and godfather. The heroes of my childhood and youth were John MacBride, Patrick Pearse and General Sean MacEoin, whom I met when I was a boy: the Blacksmith of Ballinalee whose own sweetness, honour, courage, honesty were so visible a part of him that had such a man ever met the IRA men who perpetrated the Claudy massacre in the summer of '72, he would have consigned them to the deepest circle of Dante's Inferno.

John MacBride, my granduncle, Pearse and MacEoin remain my heroes to this day. Back in 1972 in the good old days of Claudy I could see that the Provisional IRA in Northern Ireland were not in the soldierly and humanist tradition of the republican nationalism of Pearse, MacBride and MacEoin. As your Belfast Brigade and all the other northern brigades embarked upon a Thirty Years War of terror, ethnic cleansing, murder, massacre and propaganda, I felt, as a young father of two little children in Cork, inarticulate despair at what I saw as, on the one hand, the betrayal of the ideals of Pearse, MacBride and MacEoin and, on the other hand, the lethal poisoning of the atmosphere in which my children were growing up. In that sense, I did not care what the loyalist gangsters did; all I cared about was what *we* did – *we* being the republican nationalists of Ireland whose roots go back to Pearse, MacBride, MacEoin and to Davis, O'Connell, Parnell.

On a spring day early in 1990 I attended a private meeting in a house in Dublin at which you were the guest of honour and the other fifteen or so people present were an assortment of teachers, activists, clergy and journalists each of whom had opposing views to you. The purpose of the meeting was to afford you the opportunity to explain at length your point of view and for the rest of us to put our individual views to you.

At the start of the meeting, as I found myself sitting across the table from you, I found myself trembling at the sight of you. Twenty years of horror were boiling over in my soul.

One or two of the speakers lost the head but, on the whole, people were courteous and I was impressed by your willingness to listen to the other point of view.

When it came to my turn, I asked you to consider the contemporary historical context in which we were meeting. A wave of history was riding across Europe. The Berlin Wall had come down, Ceausescu had been overthrown in Romania and the dissident writer Vaslav Havel had become president in Prague. In Dublin Mary Robinson was preparing to hit out on the long road to a new presidency. Across that table on that spring day I asked you, Gerry Adams, the following question: 'In view of the great tide of history that is now riding across Europe, is this not the moment for Sinn Féin IRA to seize the historical initiative and take the loyalists, unionists, the British and Irish Governments by surprise and, at a prearranged TV rendezvous somewhere along the Border, throw down your guns and Semtex and say to your enemies, "Do your worst" or "Do your best," and in so saying throw down a gauntlet at the bar of European and world history?'

I can never forget the expression on your face as I asked you that question. Light glinting off your spectacles, you looked at me silently, whether with perplexity or pity it was impossible to know. You did not answer and the meeting went on.

And the killing went on.

Now twelve years later we have what is called a Peace Process and naturally I hope that it will succeed. But I am doubtful because I have no faith in a republican movement which turned its back on Europe in 1990 and which has never made one magnanimous gesture in the whole Thirty Years War, with the exception, of course, of Alex Maskey's recent courageous gestures as Lord Mayor of Belfast.

One of the fundamental principles of terrorism is that if it is faithfully carried out it will win, it has to win. There was no way Sinn Féin IRA could lose their war. The only question was: would they win their war in the right way? The right way meant making an imaginative, generous leap to recognise the British tradition in Ireland, but that you would not do.

If the Peace Process flickers out, it will be for two reasons: first, Sinn Féin IRA's incomprehension of the psychic darkness it has injected into the Irish soul through thirty years of terror; and second, because it is impossible to edit out of Irish history and culture the British inheritance. Sinn Féin IRA and Mrs Margaret Thatcher waged a joint war to deprive the Irish people of our inheritance of Shakespeare, the King James Bible, Milton, Handel, Jane Austen, Keats, Turner, Charles Dickens, Hopkins, Virginia Woolf, Lester Piggott, Ken Dodd, Peter Sellers, *Coronation Street*, Maggie Smith, John Hurt, Jack Charlton, David Hockney, the Ryder Cup team, the Aintree Grand National, Liverpool F.C. and Manchester United; but neither Sinn Féin nor Mrs Thatcher will ever succeed in robbing us Irish of our British inheritance. Genetically, even, vast numbers of we Irish, like Patrick Pearse himself, have English blood in our veins. My own great grandfather was Colonel Thomas Gonne, father of my grandmother Eileen and her half-sister, my grand-aunt Maud Gonne.

The paradox of politics is that politics cannot be radicalised or advanced by politics. Look at the following two famous contradictory quotations:

'In our time the destiny of man presents its meanings in political terms.' Thomas Mann, author of *The Magic Mountain.*

'History is a nightmare from which I am trying to awake.' Stephen in Joyce's *Ulysses.*

Do you see the chasm between these two statements? I believe that in 1990, if not long earlier, you and Sinn Féin IRA had the chance to rescue the peoples of Ireland and

Great Britain from the nightmare of history, but you chose not to do so and so the politics of nightmare continues.

Gerry Adams, have you ever looked at the map of the world as it was six hundred million years ago? What is now Munster, Connacht and Leinster was a landmass off the shores of Norway. Ulster was thousands of miles away and formed part of what is now Greenland and Labrador.

Politics is a game of the human animal mind. It has no basis in reality. So it was that the TV documentary series of the Peace Process was called *Endgame*. It was a well-produced documentary but I was horrified that not only you but all the participants talked about your war-games like self-absorbed schoolboys. It was all cops and robbers and John le Carré. You and Martin McGuinness and Dennis Bradley and Fred and all the rest of Mrs Thatcher's men, all of you boy scouts indulging in reminiscences of your games. You in your blue shirt and red tie and sleeves rolled up, so relaxed, so charming.

In the end, there is only the one reality: the earth itself, its climate, creatures, vegetation and rocks. Why did Sinn Féin IRA choose games – war games and word games – over the reality of life on earth?

Your Thirty Years War was not an historical inevitability. From Claudy to Enniskillen to Warrington to Canary Wharf to Omagh – not only did it betray the humane, soldierly values of Pearse, MacBride and MacEoin but also it changed this island radically from Mizen Head to Malin Head. Ireland is now a sadder and a crueller place, condemned, possibly, by your war to perpetual war. For what may the other side do but do what you did – embark on another thirty-year war of terror, 2002 AD–2032 AD?

November 27, 2002

THE THIRTY-FIFTH ANNIVERSARY
OF PATRICK KAVANAGH'S DEATH

Last Saturday, November 30 was the thirty-fifth anniversary of the death of Patrick Kavanagh, and it was commemorated by the annual Patrick Kavanagh Weekend at the Patrick Kavanagh Centre in Inniskeen, his home village in County Monaghan, three miles south of the Armagh border, half-way between Carrickmacross and Dundalk.

I drove up from Dublin on the Friday afternoon through Drogheda and Dundalk. It was a sunny, blue November afternoon and when I drove up the hill at Monasterboice there once again was that fabulous vista spread before me – the great plain of Muirthemhne and, beyond north of Inniskeen, Slieve Gullion and, to the east, the Cooley hills and the Mountains of Mourne. What a sense of homecoming Patrick Kavanagh must have felt every time he reached the crest of the hill of Monasterboice!

Inniskeen – 'Beautiful Island' – is a magically situated village on the brimming banks of the River Fane. The Fane in which Kavanagh used poach salmon rises in Lake Muckno near Castleblayney and flows down south along the Armagh border before turning left at Inniskeen and heading for the sea at Blackrock in Dundalk Bay.

I stayed the weekend down the road from the Kavanagh Centre in a B & B run by Rose Lorenz, a local woman with a heart of gold, and her kindly Rhineland chef husband, Heinz, and their two leaping and curling children, Ruth and Robert. The house like the river was full for the weekend of regulars who come back year after year to Rose's B & B, Gleneven House, for the Kavanagh weekend. Thérèse and Catherine, two sisters from Belfast, Vincent from Dublin, retired after thirty-eight years with Aer Lingus, two farmers from Bruree, Co. Limerick, Moss Kerwick and Pat Lyons, who know more about Patrick Kavanagh than most critics.

The Patrick Kavanagh Centre is located in the old Catholic church in the middle of the graveyard in which Patrick and his wife, Katherine Barry Moloney, are buried. The church has been transformed into a Kavanagh museum. The old church structure has been retained with its large upstairs galleries and a nave which is wider than it is long.

In honour of Patrick's memory we had three days of packed audiences, music, song, poetry, recollections, debates and, one of the highlights, a Commemorative Mass for Patrick Kavanagh on the Saturday night. Inniskeen's new church, the Church of Mary Mother of Mercy, is one of the most beautiful modern parish churches in Ireland, designed as a sea shell, emblem of the medieval pilgrim, by the one and only Liam McCormick.

The mass for Patrick was celebrated by the P.P. Fr Peter McGuinness with a fine choir and five-piece ensemble and the homily was by Fr Michael Murtagh, C.C. of Ardee, Co. Louth. It was a riveting homily of at least fifteen or twenty minutes but it went by in seconds. Fr Murtagh described his own childhood in Crossmaglen and fishing the lakes along the Monaghan border – 'fishing for Free State fish' as he said

– and how he became *hooked* on Kavanagh, so much so that in 1986 on the day he cleared his room in Maynooth there was only one item left in the room for his last night: *The Collected Poems of Patrick Kavanagh*. A friend not finding him in the room left a note: 'I am glad to see you have kept your bible.' Fr Murtagh observed that Kavanagh had the Three Hs: Humility which is the antidote to pride; Humour which is a sense of balance; and Holiness which is detachment or what Patrick called 'not caring'. The kindly man beside me at mass, with whom I shook hands at the Sign of Peace, had known Patrick and Katherine. He had worked in McNellos bar for forty years. Mr McCartan Comiskey.

The second highlight of the weekend was the publication of the selected prose of Patrick Kavanagh, entititled *A Poet's Country* and edited by Antoinette Quinn (The Lilliput Press, €15.00). A book of diamonds such as Kavanagh's loving account in *The Irish Times* of his visit to the Tailor and Ansty in Gougane Barra or his enchanting account in the *The Irish Press* of a reception in Áras an Uachtaráin in 1943. What the innocent Kavanagh did not know was that a file on him was kept in the Áras and it reads: 'author of some very obscene poems in English papers ... untidy and not altogether clean ... enter a caveat on his social card'. How about that – 'enter a caveat on his social card'! From 1943 until his death in 1967 Kavanagh was never again permitted to visit Áras an Uachtaráin.

The third highlight of the weekend was the bus tour on Sunday morning, in which another legendary Inniskeen man, Gene Carroll, guided us around the places made immortal by Patrick's poetry. McNello's public house with whose proprietor, Dan McNello, Patrick was great friends. Patrick often sat in McNello's living room and they used go racing together at Leopardstown. Gene told how once when Patrick's cheque for £40 bounced and Mr McNello drew Patrick's attention to this occurrence Patrick re-assured him:

'Don't worry about that – cheques have a habit of doing that. If I were you, I'd just keep presenting it.' On up Ednamo, the Inniskeen Road, Billy Brennan's Barn, Rocksavage Fort, the Plunkett-Kenny Estate, Kednaminsha School from which Patrick Kavanagh's grandfather, the schoolteacher Patrick Kevany from Easkey, Co. Sligo, was sacked because of his love affair with Kavanagh's grandmother, the beautiful Nancy Callan. Our tour ended at the Kavanagh homestead in Mucker where the poet's father played the melodeon for passers-by on their way to Christmas mass. In Inniskeen graveyard at the grave of Patrick and Katherine, Gene Carroll recited the poem 'Peace'. The wreath, tied with bullwire by Peter Murphy, was laid by a big Dublin man called Patrick Kavanagh who played lock forward for Lansdowne Rugby Club in the 1950s. I thought of how the poet Patrick Kavanagh loved to watch rugby games on TV and how he loved the expression 'The Irish forwards have it'; in company with Katherine Moloney in a bar, Patrick loved to exclaim 'Moloney has it.'

Last time I was in Inniskeen graveyard, in 1994, there was a beautiful standing stone carved by the distinguished sculptor Tom Glendon to the memory of Patrick and Katherine, but at Patrick's old home I found a grave with a small wooden cross to the memory of Patrick only. I was nonplussed for it seemed Patrick was buried in his old front garden in Mucker while his wife was buried a mile away in Inniskeen. In August 1998, a few days before the Omagh bombing, I heard a report on RTÉ News that men had come in the night to Inniskeen graveyard and taken away the beautiful stone and hammered it into bits. The stone with its Maltese cross and its porthole window to the sky reflected Patrick Kavanagh's unique kind of Zen Christianity. Such a queer and fearful thing to have stolen and hammered into bits: the carved headstone of your own native poet.

Debate turned on the question of whether Patrick

Kavanagh was a mystic. Sr Una Agnew and Fr Tom Stack saw Kavanagh as a mystic. John McArdle's passionately sceptical voice expressed fears that the kind of religion which Patrick repudiated in his essay 'Sex and Christianity' might now be colonising the dead poet's work – a view which prefigured the same point made by Fr Michael Murtagh in his homily when he quoted Kavanagh to the effect that 'the dead will wear the cap of any racket'. John Moriarty in a harrowing presentation saw Patrick Kavanagh as a 'visionary', not a mystic.

The last event was the presentation by Rosaleen Kearney of the Annual Patrick Kavanagh Award, which went to Alice Lyons of Cootehall – that fabled, dark, bright quarter of County Roscommon. Alice Lyons was over the moon, and I know just how she felt for since I myself was given the same award in 1974 I have stayed the far side of the moon.

I drove back to Dublin through the night by Louth village, Ardee, Slane, Kilmoone, Finglas; the same route Patrick took when, in December 1931, he first walked to Dublin. I dropped off John Moriarty on the quays and I drove out the river to Ringsend.

Poet of Dublin city as well as of Inniskeen, Patrick Kavanagh was the funniest as well as the kindest poet I have ever known. But he hated Nice in the South of France, where friends took him on holiday in the summer of 1956. Back in Dublin in McDaids bar he used pretend to be a District Justice: 'Ye blackguard ye! If I've said it once, I've said it a hundred times. If I see you in this court again, you can expect not less than three weeks in Nice. D'ye hear me? Ye blackguard ye! Not less than three weeks in Nice!'

December 4, 2002

THE MANY WOMEN OF RINGSEND AND
THE ONE WOMAN OF SANDYMOUNT

I live in Ringsend, which is the first of three villages on the south shore of Dublin Bay where the Liffey meets the sea: Ringsend, Irishtown and Sandymount; and in the hinterland the fourth village, landlocked Ballsbridge, which, before it became a compound of the affluent, was an old Dublin working-class village. My first neighbour in Ringsend, the late Mr William Rafferty, was a retired coachbuilder from Ballsbridge whose dignity, when I first landed into Ringsend eighteen years ago, I capsized by addressing him as a Ringsender. 'I am not a Ringsender,' he yelled. 'I am a Ballsbridger.' He had married a Ringsender, but although he resided in Ringsend he would always be a Ballsbridger and he was shocked that I had mistaken him for a Ringsender. William Rafferty is long gone home to God but, in spite of the passing years and the Celtic Tiger, the integrity of the old villages survives by a few threads. In the last four weeks there have been two daring unveilings of street sculpture, one in Ringsend and one in Sandymount.

Monday last week at noon, in blasted cold and pouring sunlight, on the island at the Library on Irishtown Road in the heart of Ringsend village, Gráinne Healy, Chairperson of the National Women's Council, unveiled a life-size sculpture of a door. Made by Siobhán Geoghegan, it was conceived by the Domestic Violence Group under the wing of the Ringsend Action Project (RAP) as Ringsend's contribution to the 16 Days of Action on Violence Against Women National Campaign. The Door – painted black and white because domestic violence is a black-and-white issue – embodies and symbolises that most domestic violence occurs behind closed doors. The Door embodies and symbolises captivity and liberation. One side of the door is stamped with the language of violence: 'PLEADING'; 'BROKEN BONES'; 'FORCED SEX'. The other side of the door is stamped with the words of liberation: 'NOT ALONE'; 'STARTING OVER'; 'SMALL VICTORIES'. The Door is slightly ajar, embodying and symbolising that it is possible for the victim to open the door and seek freedom and help.

The Lord Mayor of Dublin, Dermot Lacey, made a passionate speech in which he expressed his shame and shock at the terrible statistics of violence against women as outlined by the Project manager, Aileen Foran, and by Catherine Gorman of The Women of the Door: eighty-three women murdered in Ireland since 1996, mostly by men who knew their victims – husbands, partners, boyfriends, acquaintances. Lord Mayor Lacey observed that, notwithstanding, males also are beneficiaries of the women's movement.

Watched by a large crowd including Ringsend Community Garda Kevin Byrne, Ruairí Quinn (Labour), Eoin Ryan (Fianna Fáil), Daithí Doolan (Sinn Féin) – there was no Fine Gael representative – Joe Grennell (Aileen Foran's colleague in the Ringsend Action Project) and the parish priest, Fr Michael Coady. Gráinne Healy, like some young age-old Celtic priestess, untied the red ribbon around the white shroud and unveiled the door. From across the road watched that gentleman of style Mr Shay Keller in Carlisle Cleaners, the man in Skidmarks Auto Parts, the butchers in Clynes Meats and the men in yellow hats and hi-viz vests on the top storey of the scaffolding of the new block a-building on Ropewalk Place. Never was 'DOORNESS' more felt by and visible to the women who made it and the men who helped them.

The ceremony ended with Ringsend woman Mary Dent in buckskin jacket and blue jeans singing with real feeling Jimmy McCarthy's poem-song, 'Bright Blue Rose'. Juggernauts and four-wheel drives were roaring past and a strong wind was blowing in the freezing sunlight, but Mary Dent's every grace-note could be heard.

Alas, the door is not a permanent fixture as it has only temporary permission from Dublin City Council.

The second daring unveiling of street sculpture was in Sandymount three weeks earlier. At 2 p.m. on a cold, dark Wednesday afternoon the President of Mexico, Vicente Fox, rode up Sandymount strand on a grey mare and reined her in at the sea wall at the Irishtown end of the promenade. Actually, of course, he rode up in a blue limousine. A local woman exclaimed: 'O my God, isn't he drop-dead gorgeous!' I would need to be a de-testosteroned politically correct geek not to have agreed with her. El Presidente de Mexico Licentiad, Vicente Fox, is the full Mexican peso. As he ambled along the lines of two coach-loads of Mexican students, tall and ruggedly handsome, he looked like a cross between the young Jack Nicholson and Clark Gable in his prime. Dressed but not overdressed. A cool dude, a man of style who does not descend to the ostentatious. A hint of the inscrutable romantic.

Ahead of him at the top of the promenade awaited a thirty-foot-high steel sculpture, painted white, whose sections had been assembled and riveted in the previous weeks; a creation of the Mexican sculptor Enrique Carvajal, alias Sebastian, from Chihuahua in north-central Mexico.

When I first set eyes on this sculpture, I was shocked, as one naturally is by something new in a familiar landscape. I have been a daily communicant for eighteen years on the promenade at Sandymount. The sudden appearance one day of this tall White Lady stopped me in my tracks. At first I was angry that my familiar perspective had been, as I saw it, intruded upon. All the ignorance and philistinism of my innate human savagery, which I share with everyone else, roared up inside me and I condemned it in the supreme court of my tiny mind. But as time went by and day followed day the White Lady of Sandymount began to grow on me until this morning, on my way to the Radio Centre at RTÉ in that other landlocked village of Donnybrook, I recognised her for who she is – a creature of beauty. Finest of fine lines, finest of fine features, fine art. Seen from city-side in the west, she is a White Lady from Chihuahua howling on the seafront at Sandymount, waiting for her Irish sailor boy – Jim Joyce probably – to come home to her from across the Irish Sea. Although she is white as opposed to brown, you can see the Aztec signature in the steel plates of her howling.

The White Lady has been my own name for her until yesterday when the Mexican Ambassador, Agustin Basave, kindly e-mailed me to say that the sculptor's original name for her when he made her eighteen months ago was – guess what? – 'The White Lady'! *Mujer Blanca*. So the White Lady she was, and is, the White Lady of Sandymount.

Behind the White Lady stood a small white marquee erected for the convenience of President Vicente Fox and his party by a Dublin City Council official who had obviously been studying the paintings of the renowned Mexican woman painter Frida Kahlo. Over it soared three flagpoles – Ireland, Mexico and the City of Dublin. Another on-the-ball City Council official had acquired from Bargain Stores the longest red carpet I have ever seen and laid it over a spread of bark-mould, which discreetly solved the problem of the mucky ground. The No. 1 Garda Band warmed us all up with pride and zest: 'Explosion'; 'Mexico'; 'South of the Border'; and 'Come into the Parlour'. Sandymount Community Garda Derek Dempsey kept an eye on proceedings from the corner of Gilford Road and remarked that he for one liked the new sculpture.

Again the Lord Mayor of Dublin, Dermot Lacey, spoke, standing, as he always does in fierce cold, without an overcoat out of respect for the occasion. President Vicente Fox did wear an overcoat, a blue lambswool, and spoke in sumptuously broken English and unveiled the plaque for, of course, the White Lady herself was not veiled. For several days already, she had been standing naked to the four winds as she always will. The plaque reads:

> *A Gift from Mexico to Ireland*
> *Unveiled by President Vicente Fox*
> *On November 13 2002*

But whether she too will be removed like the door in Ringsend remains to be seen. One Sandymount woman while acknowledging, as she put it, the 'elegance' of the White Lady, added: 'She should be down in Kerry where she belongs!' The question, I suppose, is: is Sandymount in Ireland? Is Ringsend in Ireland? Indeed, is Kerry in Ireland? That is the question, Gertie, that is the question.

December 11, 2002

AMERICA, IRELAND AND IRAQ

We Irish are in love with the United States of America for the good reason that American culture is part of our own culture: Hollywood, McDonalds, Disneyland, Pepsodent, Elvis Presley, Frank Sinatra, Muhammad Ali, Tiger Woods, Marilyn Monroe, Hemingway, Ella Fitzgerald, Bob Dylan, advertising, television, skyscrapers, shopping malls, guns, the electric chair, baseball caps, baseball bats (ouch), trainers, t-shirts, teddy bears, denim, crew-cuts, chewing gum, Budweiser, Ford Motors, *Time* magazine, *Newsweek*, Coca Cola and – Santa Claus. We set such store by American standards that we consider that an Irish citizen has not really made it unless he or she has made it in the USA: Tony O'Reilly, Pierce Brosnan, Gerry Adams, U2, Seamus Heaney, Riverdance, Frank Patterson, Frank McCourt, the Clancy Brothers, the Chieftains. Naturally, therefore, if at the end of the Third World War into which the USA is whipping us the empire of the USA collapses, we will grieve even if we escape the physical holocaust. Much of what we love, and are a part of, will disappear and die and we will look back in sorrow and lament the passing of a world we loved.

I say 'the empire' of the USA. Oddly the US Government does not style and promote itself as an empire and yet it is the largest and most successful empire in the history of mankind. The British empire was proud to be known as the British Empire, as was the Roman Empire in a province of which the Jewish Palestinian dissident Jesus Christ was born. The word 'empire' comes from the Latin 'imperium'. The Roman Empire was the *Imperium Romanum*.

But the USA continues to refuse to acknowledge itself as being an 'empire' and its presidents, although comporting themselves as emperors, do not permit themselves to be addressed as emperors.

When I was a child General Eisenhower was Military Governor. But he was succeeded by the young Emperor John F. Kennedy whom we in Ireland idolised. In recent times we have seen two spectacular American emperors: the big, tall cowboy Emperor Reagan and the golden-jawed, chromium-nosed Emperor Clinton. And now we are living in the reign of another lean, tall cowboy, Emperor Bush.

The US is loath to style itself as an 'empire' because it knows that empires are by definition doomed. Because an empire by definition infects the nations which it colonises, the empire's own soul is contaminated and, in its deepest bowels, breeds cancer cells for which in history there is no known cure; a type of cancer that was known to the Greeks as hubris. The *Chambers Dictionary* defines hubris as 'arrogance, such as invites disaster'.

The war in Iraq in particular and the twin general wars on Islam and the Third World are a last throw of the dice by the US Empire to save itself from its own cancer. It can end only in destruction; not only of Iraq and Palestine and Israel and Saudi Arabia and chunks of Asia, Africa and South America but also of the USA itself and, therefore, of course, of our young State here in Ireland. If our children survive the Third World War and live to see the smoking ruin of what's left of the world, they will inhabit a cultural as well as a physical landscape of which we today have no concept.

A great empire like the USA is confronted by the tragedy of its own shadow in the world, which explains why American emperors are hooked on the word 'evil'. The Emperor Reagan liked to speak of what he called 'the Empire of Evil' (meaning Russia) and the Emperor Bush likes to speak of the 'the Axis of Evil' (meaning Iran, North Korea, Iraq and Cuba – Cuba of where Dr David Hickey, Head of Renal Transplant Surgery in Beaumont Hospital, stated on RTÉ TV a fortnight ago that, if he was terminally ill, he'd prefer to be than Ireland because Cuba, in spite of the US Empire, has a more humane and fair health service than the US or Ireland). Indeed, the Emperor Bush uses the word 'evil' with such frequency that one wonders about the state of his own soul. If one invited him to supper, how often would he use the word 'evil'?

And if the Emperor Bush did come around here to supper in Ringsend, if he was not in his cowboy hat and black leather gloves, what kind of casual clothes would he be wearing? Would he come in fashionable gear? In a bold, black headline on December 7, *The Irish Times* summed up what is hip this Christmas: IMPOVERSIHED LOOK HAS A WEALTH OF FASHION DEVOTEES. What could more memorably sum up the achievement of the US Empire than to be able to report that here in Ireland – 'in de lil' ol' emerald isle' – the Impoverished Look is in! Our great problem in Ireland is part of the greater problem that is eating up the soul of the US Empire. Greed.

The supreme value in Ireland now, as in the US, is money: what you own and how much you spend. An enthusiastic businessman explained to me: 'Greed, Paul, greed is the problem in Ireland and the only solution is to spread the greed around more evenly. An even spread of greed would solve our problem.' A man, surely, after the Emperor Bush's heart. A man with a philosophy of greed. He himself takes fishing holidays in Siberia and sun holidays with the wife in the Maldives. 'You don't know the Maldives? Ah for heaven's sake, surely you know the Maldives. The Maldives that's off the coast of India ... there's nothing to beat the Maldives ... the wife found them ... she found the Maldives on the Internet ... she's phenomenal on the Internet, the wife ... shopping on the web ... only yesterday she bought a handbag on the web for €400 and she was ecstatic!'

The same man has two – sometimes three – of everything: two cars, two boats, three houses, two gardeners, three TV sets, three computers, two holidays, two children; two or three of everything. And the philosopher of greed sees himself, as does the Emperor Bush, as a Christian when in fact his philosophy of greed has no more in common with Christianity than the Emperor Bush's philosophy of war.

The original, historical, Jewish Palestinian dissident Jesus of Nazareth, as well as the legendary Christ of the early churches, was an uncompromising pacifist. He told his peoples that the greatest evil is war. The world of smart bombs, bunker-buster bombs, thermobaric bombs, microwave bombs is a world of pure, shining, virginal evil. And yet the Emperor Bush pronounces himself a Christian and in his campaign to prosecute a Third World War he invokes the God of Christianity. Understandably the ordinary Muslim like myself in my cave or yourself in the bazaar or at home in the cardboard shed with the telly takes the Emperor at his word and interprets the Third World War as a war waged by a fanatical Christian emperor.

Nor could your ordinary Muslim be expected to know that Irish lateral thinking is part of the war strategy of the US Empire. Yet since November 28, Black Thursday, the day the National Spatial Strategy was announced at the Irish Museum of Modern Art, the White House has been buzzing with the Spatial Strategy plan for Iraq. 'Baghdad is no longer to be a Gateway; Baghdad is to be a Hub. Same goes for Basra. Basra, you will be a hub and not a gateway. We will open up Strategic Linking Corridors in southern Iraq and Strategic Radial Corridors in Western Iraq. We will decentralise the desert and we will create Growth Poles along the Euphrates and the Tigris. Our war cry will be: GATEWAYS and HUBS! HUBS and GATEWAYS! PEOPLE! PLACES! POTENTIAL! And the Garden of Eden will be transferred from the Department of the Environment to the Department of Arts, Sports and Tourism under its new Minister, Condoleeza Rice, Sinn Féin TD for Kerry North.'

In the holocaust to come, no Muslim or Arab will ever know that in Ireland we speak the same language as the language of the Empire of the United States of America.

Isn't that so, George Walker Bush? Be it Dublin or Dallas, it's the same ball park, the same hardball, the same toast, the same bottom line, the same lingo of money, destruction and death. By the waters of Babylon, I sat down and wept, stood up and was vaporised by a smart bomb.

December 18, 2002

MR CHARLES HAUGHEY

A few days before Christmas, in Dublin city centre in a crowded restaurant at lunchtime, I chanced to bump into Mr Charles Haughey. After a short, snatched conversation, partly in Irish, we went our different ways. Regrettably I cannot call myself a friend of Mr Haughey. I say 'regrettably' because that is something I would have relished – Mr Haughey's friendship. However, a long time ago, I did a have a brief professional relationship with Mr Haughey and, as I walked off down O'Connell Street past the first section of the Spire and over the bridge and down the quays, I mused on that piece of business all of sixteen years ago.

1986, March, a cold dark afternoon in my cave in Ringsend, the phone rang. 'My name is Catherine Butler. I am Mr Haughey's secretary. Will you speak to Mr Haughey?' I had never had any contact with Mr Haughey in my life, good, bad or indifferent, but, being a trueborn Irish Roman Catholic, an arrow of guilt flew through my soul. What crime had I committed to merit a phone call

from the former and future Taoiseach and Leader of Fianna
Fáil?

'Paul, I'd like you to come in and see me.'

Over the phone he offered no explanation and I made no
inquiry. A few days later I found myself sitting in the empty
Fianna Fáil meeting-room on the fifth floor of Leinster
House. I sat facing a wall with a large, dark, wintry Paul
Henry painting.

Mr Haughey came in and we talked for an hour and what
surprised me then but does not now, on recollection, was his
diffidence; his open-ended, quizzical, risky approach to the
project he had in mind. He informed me that the official
opening of Knock International Airport was due to take place
in two months time, on May 30, and that he had been asked
to perform the official opening. He did not say, as I later
learned, that he was being invited in preference to the
incumbent Taoiseach, Garrett FitzGerald, because the people
of Knock and the people of Mayo, including Fine Gael
people, felt that Mr Haughey had supported them through
thick and thin to get Knock International Airport built in the
face of contemptuous opposition from every quarter, most
especially from the pedigree economists, calculators and
sophists of Dublin and the Pale.

What Mr Haughey wanted from me was advice about the
feasibility of some kind of memorial to mark the birth of
Knock International Airport. He said he had been thinking
of Raftery – Raftery *an file* – Raftery the poet of Mayo, but
that he had not got any definite proposal. What did I think?
Maybe a quotation from Raftery on a slab of Mayo
limestone? A quotation from which poem? Or did I think it
would be possible to compose original lines? And if new lines
could be produced should they be read out at the official
opening and, if so, by whom should they be read out – by the
author of the lines or by an actor or by whom? The
conversation went to and fro, probing here, withdrawing

there. Mr Haughey stood at a window overlooking Kildare Street, with his knee on a chair. I thought to myself: what a breath of fresh air to see a politician thinking aloud, trying to open up all the possibilities of a situation. This was a new experience for me, all too accustomed as I was to people in power whose minds had closed up at puberty and who worked only in terms of votes and certainties and who would regard it as criminal to think freely and to take risks.

After a good hour of looking at the problem, Mr Haughey asked me if I would accept a commission to write a poem for the opening of Knock International Airport and to recite the poem from the platform on the day. I accepted and Mr Haughey called in Mr Pádraig Flynn who, he said, would give me any help I might need. Mr Flynn was the soul of goodwill and good humour and as we rode down the elevator together I thought how refreshing to be in a lift with a politician who is on his way into the first chamber of parliament to make a speech against divorce – a position absolutely opposed to my own – and who yet treats me with courtesy. Furthermore, looking at the Knock Poem project from Mr Flynn's point of view, I knew that the proposal could only prove a nuisance to him. I know County Mayo well – my mother and father were from Westport and Turlough – and I knew that the Knock opening would be hard trucking. But now poor Mr Flynn had to go back to his Fianna Fáil Cumann in Castlebar and inform them that the Boss, would ye believe it, has landed us with a poet, and guess who the poet is, one of the bleddy Free State Durcans! That Paul Durcan lootheramaun; a string of a fella with white Nike trainers and long hair. As Mr Flynn strode toward the chamber, I thought, by God but whoever it was who said that courtesy is the first commandment was right.

On the morning of the big day I was to be at Mr Haughey's residence at Kinsealy for 11.30 a.m. Mr Haughey himself answered the door, showed me into a drawing room, asked me what would I like to drink and went away. At 1 p.m. Mr Haughey called me to join him and Mrs Haughey in a car to drive to Dublin Airport. The driver had taped the 1 p.m. news and he played it back to Mr Haughey in the passenger seat. The lead news was Jim Fahy in Knock reporting that it was lashing rain and crashing gales. No one in the car spoke. At a roundabout a woman driver obeyed the rules of the roundabout and Mr Haughey leaned forward and saluted her. I was astonished that a man whose day was in ruins before it had even started should be concerned with such chivalry.

At Dublin Airport I climbed aboard a seven-seater plane: myself and Mr P. J. Mara crouched in the tail, Mr Haughey with his back to me and Mrs Haughey and, facing them, Mr Brian Lenihan looking appallingly ill, his face a whiter shade of white, and yet as the small plane was tossed up into the skies over County Dublin it was he who had the nerve not only to speak but to make a wise crack. Grimacing, and glancing down derisively at terra firma, Brian Lenihan sighed: 'The Party can live on our martyrdom for the next hundred years.'

I like flying but this was a hairy flight. We had to fly so low and at such almost upside-down angles that I got close-up views of cattle huddling under hedges and of the slates on Longford cathedral. I was terrified not that we were going to crash but that I was going to vomit all over Mr Haughey. The pilot shouted: 'Control says we're three minutes early – will I circle or go straight in?' Mr Haughey murmured: 'Straight in.'

The storm was such that half the platform had blown away; yet the plain people of Mayo, drenched to their bones, greeted Mr Haughey as a saviour, just as in the 1880s they had greeted Maud Gonne as a saviour when that pale, young Englishwoman attended evictions and stood herself between the cottage door and the bailiff's battering ram.

In the tiny airport building the crowd was so tight I

thought that my back would be broken. An unknown hand gripped my hand and it was Mr Haughey and he insisted on making a way for me through the pack so that he could introduce me to Monsignor Horan, the original begetter of Knock International Airport. Again, another apparently unnecessary gesture on the part of Mr Haughey. Down the sixteen years that have elapsed I have thought: who else but he would have bothered?

As we gathered to return to Dublin, Mr Haughey announced that he was taking the helicopter to Inishvickillane. Mr Bertie Ahern was aghast. He remonstrated with Mr Haughey regarding the foul weather. Mr Haughey replied: 'If it gets too bad we can always put down.'

'Put down where?' cried Mr Ahern.

'In a field,' Mr Haughey replied.

In that city-centre restaurant before Christmas, as I bade farewell to Mr Haughey in his blue blazer and open-necked shirt, I saw again that Mr Haughey is a traveller-king of ship or plane, officially retired but actually still on his feet at the wheel of the open seas, the open skies of life and death.

January 22, 2003

THE FUNERAL OF TONY O'MALLEY

Driving into the egg-slicer narrow streets of Callan, Co. Kilkenny last Friday morning for the 10.30 a.m. funeral of Tony O'Malley, I am ashamed to confess that I could not lick my addiction to newsprint and I stopped at the first newsagent, Hacketts on the left side of Bridge Street. The young newsagent spoke warmly of Tony O'Malley as a storyteller, especially about people and their families. 'He knew all about who was related to who and the whole family history.' I bought a bottle of water to mitigate the sin of the newspaper under my arm. As I left, Mr Hackett mentioned that the house next door was Tony O'Malley's original home, where his mother had a grocery shop and from where his Clare Island father used travel for Singer sewing machines.

Although it was only 9.45 a.m. multitudes were arriving at the church. The celebrant, Fr Patrick O'Brien from Co. Mayo, was walking up the street with the poet Brian Lynch, editor of the great book of O'Malley entitled *Tony O'Malley* (Kilkenny, 1996).

Inside the church door, on the table of offerings, lay Tony O'Malley's accordion, a hurling stick signed by the Kilkenny team and one of his palettes and brushes.

Up at the altar rail on the left stood Tony O'Malley's open coffin – thank God not lidded yet – and, lo and behold, there was the eighty-nine-year-old rebel himself stretched out like a feather in repose in his battered old working sunhat, blue shirt, blue jumper, rosary beads, a pair of baggy green corduroy pants, blue shoes and, in the crook of his left arm, his adored wife Jane's wedding bouquet of sea-pink from thirty years ago. Tony O'Malley and Jane Harris married July 10, 1973.

The bird of his soul had not yet flown the nest of his body – that amphibious eye, that ring-a-ring of roses smile, those harmonica-kissing lips, all that good nature. And between his feet a toy, marmalade kitten, placed there by one of his Canadian grandnieces.

At Tony O'Malley's shoulder stood the painter Brian Bourke making a last sketch – his two hands working like a potato-digger, all concentration on the task in hand, the necessary, natural task in hand. Thirty years ago Bourke stood in the wings of the Olympia theatre sketching Marcel Marceau and now here he was sketching another great abstract mime artist who seemed to be saying to us as we peered down at him: 'Don't mind me – carry on. I am enjoying myself.' In spite of the unbearable grief of his parting from us all, most of all from his wife Jane, never can a man be said to have so visibly enjoyed his own funeral mass. In those last minutes before the lidding of the coffin, it was like a painting by Tony O'Malley himself; not only a painting but a *construction* (how he loved the word *construction*), a Russian construction that out-Chagalled Chagall, out-Maleviched Malevich. In the Church of the Assumption in Callan, Co. Kilkenny we were seeing with our own eyes the assumption of Tony O'Malley into heaven. As earthy, as innocent a human being that ever walked the earth.

The coffin was lidded and the dignitaries arrived: the aide-de-camp to President McAleese, Col. Traolach Young; the Mayor of Kilkenny City, Cllr Betty Manning; and the members of Kilkenny City Borough Council in their red and black robes, Cambro-Normans all. I could not help tracing one councillor's skull, just as Tony O'Malley used do, with his forefinger, the Norman effigies of Kilkenny. Tony O'Malley was a Freeman of Kilkenny City.

The two-hour Mass itself was a Russian as well as Roman mass. Chants of praise, incense and passion, all grandeur and simplicity, all lectern and iconostasis, the celebrant and his five concelebrants, including Professor Enda McDonagh of Maynooth, all wearing the white and gold vestments of the resurrection. The Kilkenny Choir in the gallery pouring forth hymns in Latin; poets, philosophers, musicians, family pouring forth praise.

Ellen O'Malley read from the Tao:

> *True perfection seems imperfect,*
> *Yet it is perfectly itself.*

In his homily Fr O'Brien quoted the Jewish philosopher Abraham Heschel that there are three stages of mourning: tears, silence, song. Fr O'Brien spoke to the grief of Jane O'Malley and how in their marriage she and Tony 'gave each other new life'. He spoke of the silence of Tony's paintings and of 'the silence of the contemplation of generations to come' as they look at Tony's works. Fr O'Brien depicted the musical notation of Tony O'Malley's paintings. Fr O'Brien spoke of the song of Tony O'Malley's conversation, of its all-around-Clare Island digressions. Fr O'Brien said: 'The music of his voice was the timbre of friendship.'

Gerry O'Malley said: 'Cousin Tony was the most honest man I have ever known.' Seamus Heaney, appearing like a chevalier in a snowstorm, read *The Windhover* by Father Hopkins.

In his 1999 birthday poem for Tony O'Malley, Brian Lynch spoke of 'that pebble solitude, the cornerstone he built upon'.

At the Consecration Fr O'Brien broke the bread of the Eucharist and held out before us the two wings of the Host. The mass rose up into the climax of the Eucharist itself when the County Mayo priest not only invited but encouraged, implored, yet in no way coerced, everyone, all four hundred of us, to come to the altar, to come to the communion table and partake of the meal. Father O'Brien stood there at the altar, his two hands held out, his two arms embracing us all; he stood there like a fisherman on the shores of Galilee, the shores of Clare Island, urging, yet not compelling, all our boats to come in, all our frail currachs to come in on the wave of the peace of Tony O'Malley. Fr O'Brien was like a mother hen shepherding her chicks, a father rounding up his calves. Almost the whole church answered his call to join the poet Jesus and the painter Tony to break bread at the table of peace. The word *peace* was heard so often during this mass that it sounded like a new word never uttered before, or like an old word that made the world's headlines of war seem so stupid, stupid.

People asked: who is this priest? I thought: if only Fr Patrick O'Brien of the Archdiocese of Tuam were a Bishop, what a light he would be in this dark time, in this 'Good Friday time' as Tony O'Malley would have called it.

And I thought also: here we are, four hundred ordinary Iraqi folk gathered in Callan under Slievenamon to bury our *saoi*, our wise man, Tony O'Malley. Wouldn't it be so typical of the Americans or the British to drop a bomb on this church and call it an accident?

After communion Maya Homburger on violin and Malcolm Proud at harpsichord played the Largo from the Sonata in C Minor by Bach.

In his eulogy John O'Donohue, author of *Anam Cara*, told us about that phrase in Connemara which says: *bhí nádúir ann*. Meaning: he was a man of nature, an affectionate man. *Bhí nádúir ann*. And he added: *Duine uasal a bhí ann*. Tony O'Malley was a noble person.

The Chairman of the Arts Council, Patrick Murphy from New Ross, made the speech that crowned it all; it lasted but seconds; a soft-spoken cry of friendship that ended in tears. Nora Ring sang out the bearers under the pall of the feather of their dead chieftain.

In the ancient cemetery of Kilbride on the Tipperary border – where, as Tony O'Malley's neighbour the poet Michael Coady of Carrick-on-Suir pointed out to me, Amhlaiodh Ó Súilleabháin (died 1838), the first Gaelic diarist, is also buried – Tony O'Malley was laid down under avenues of clipped yews. Fr O'Brien – facing south to the grave under him and, beyond, Slievenamon skirted in white mists of thousands of white doves from the dovecote of the garden in Physicianstown where Tony and Jane lived and worked and had their being – led us in a decade of the Mystery of Good Friday.

After Jane's niece Karen read a valedictory Bahamanian poem for Tony, the mourners led out by one of the O'Malley women raised up Patrick Pearse's song:

> *Oró sé do bheatha 'bhaile*
> *Oró sé do bheatha 'bhaile*
> *Oró sé do bheatha 'bhaile*
> *Anois ar theacht an tsamhraidh*
>
> *Ta Gráinne Mhaol ag teacht thar sáile*
> *Óglaigh armtha léi mar gharda*
> *Gaeil iad féin is ní Gaill ná Spáinnigh*
> *Is cuirfidh siad ruaig ar Ghallaibh.*

January 29, 2003

NEWFOUNDLAND 1

This day two weeks ago, Ash Wednesday, March 5, I awake in the city of St John's, capital of Newfoundland – that torso of an island off the shores of north-east Quebec, the size of England, Scotland and Wales, the island at the end of the Brendan Voyage – to blue skies, sunlight, steep hill streets of clapboard houses painted red, green, blue, yellow, banked with eight to twelve feet of snow and ice and temperatures of -10 to -30ºC.

I have an early breakfast of eggs Benedict and whole-wheat toast, chatting with Jan Peters, landlady of my B & B, the Prescott Inn, one of the top B & Bs in the world, the equal of Pouso Chico Rei in Ouro Preto in Brazil or Gray's Guest House on Achill Island.

At 9 a.m. I am headed up the hill towards the Basilica of St John the Baptist, hoping to catch the 9.30 a.m. mass. The sidewalks are rutted with ice so there is no choice but to walk on the salted and gritted street. Still, I have to pick my steps. One false step and I will be on my face with a broken ankle.

Every time a car appears I halt. Not as hazardous as it sounds: in Newfoundland pedestrians have right of way and that's not the law, that's a way of life, that's Newfoundland etiquette.

Passers-by look me in the eye and say 'Hi'. This also is Newfoundland custom; people in the cities and town make eye contact and say 'Hi'; a shock to the likes of myself who hail from the cold, cold streets of Dublin City of the Eyes Averted.

The Basilica of St John the Baptist in the city of St John is one of the temples of the world: ornate, vast, tragic. Down the hill is Mount Cashel, the Christian Brothers orphanage whence in the 1980s came the first revelations in the Western World of child abuse.

Built by the Irish in the 1840s, the Basilica is perched astride the most strategic hill in the city. How did Bishop Fleming manage that? The British Crown said to him: you can have whatever land you can clear and fence in one night. So all the Irish labourers of St John's and the Avalon Peninsula raced to the hill and all night they laboured as they'd never laboured before until by dawn they had cleared and fenced the most stony but most beautiful vantage point in the city.

I stand on the steps of the Basilica looking down into the Harbour and feast my eyes on the thin-lipped mouth of the Narrows – a sliver of white-capped choppy water between two snowed-up headlands offering entry to the harbour.

When I stagger inside from the snow, ice and sun, there are already crowds shifting about, saying the Stations of the Cross. *Déjà-vu*. All the faces are Irish, albeit sixth generation. I could be in Enniscorthy or Westport. Folk are even dressed like the ordinary faithful of Ireland. Men in shiny suits, blazers, slacks. Big, matronly, wide-thighed ladies in red jumpers and long black skirts and golden rinse hair-dos. Only, these folk here are more relaxed and friendly than we are. At the Sign of Peace they are eager to shake hands, smile, laugh. Social integrity in contrast to the disintegration of Irish society coarsened by the cult of money, status, celebrity.

Ash Wednesday Mass is celebrated by the P.P. Fr Barton, a local man in his fifties who trained in All Hallows in Dublin. Slumped, head bowed, in his chair far up on the altar of the temple with its maroon and deep green ceiling, he radiates serious humility. He speaks simply, sparely. The Gospel, Matthew 6: 1–18, is Donal McCann scolding churchgoers on our hypocrisy; only Donal never named his source.

After mass I go in search of a brochure of the Basilica. I fetch up in the innards, in the sacristy, talking to Mr Coady from the souvenir shop and the sacristan, Mr Jack Fardy, and his helpers, Mr Boyle (a dead ringer for an older Mr P. J. Mara) and Mr Donovan, Mr Costigan, Mr McGann and his wife, Rose Marie Clooney.

At 11.30 a.m. I creep off down the hill to near the harbour front in the city centre, Water Street. In Coffee and Co., a real coffee shop with snugs, I sip at a tall latté. Oooh! I glance at *The Globe and Mail*, Canada's main daily. The editorial page carries an article by Harvard lawyer Alan Dershowitz with the headline: 'THE CASE FOR TORTURING KHALID SHAIKK MOHAMMED' – Osama Bin Laden's right-hand man, allegedly 'snatched' in Rawalpindi two days ago. I do *not* read it. We know from the *New York Times* that the US practises the most evil forms of torture and that Little Boy George is the real barbarian inside the gates. Everyone in Newfoundland regards Bush as a little boy who wants to urinate on Baghdad and cry 'Daddy, look at me! Yippee!'

The great restorative of travel and working abroad is that it shocks the system into true perspective and names like Rumsfeld, Perle, Cheney, Straw, Rice, Powell, Hoon, Negroponte, Bush, Wolfowtiz, Kissinger and Tommy Franks sound even more grotesque and ludicrous than usual.

Next morning, Thursday March 6, I travel to Corner Brook on the other side of Newfoundland. The plan is to go by road via Gander but the Mounties (the RCMP) inform us that the highway is too dangerous. Heavy snow, big winds, temperatures of -30 to -40ºC. We fly to Deer Lake, which is only one hour's drive from Corner Brook, in an Air Labrador eighteen-seater with two propellers. Drawling laconic safety instructions, the flight attendant requests us six passengers to try and not scrape the paint if we are evacuating onto the wings.

Descending into Deer Lake we crash into turbulence but the pilot makes a spot-on landing and I congratulate him and he thanks me. Happily, in this time of American-induced hysteria, the pilot left the cockpit door open.

Friday – between two poetry-music events – I walk around a frozen-over lake through snowed up birch and fir, pine and dogwood. The path is concealed under snow and, either side of it, the snow is twelve feet deep but my minder, Nick Avis, knows the way and I only fall three or four times. On slopes he takes me by the hand and drags me up. To take a photo I take off a glove and in thirty seconds my fingers freeze.

Back in the hotel, my cheeks sting sweetly and my soul is purged.

On Saturday before the night recital, we drive out thirty miles to the actual coast at Lark Harbour. Along part of the road is exposed the ocean floor of 480 million years ago. How about that, Little Boy George? 480 million years old! You and lil' ol' Condo Rice and lil' ol' Don 'Rummy' Rumsfeld oughta hop uppa here and lay your heads down on this lil' ol' ocean floor. 480 million years might cure you of your sickness. Lark Harbour is an ancient outport on the Gulf of St Lawrence where the sea is all frozen over and I pretend to be Tom Crean in Antarctica and I think of my daughter Síabhra and her husband Blaise back in Ballymahon who revere Tom Crean and Ernest Shackleton.

Corner Brook is also a ski resort and on Sunday afternoon

I am taken to Marble Mountain, fifteen minutes drive from the town centre, and, borrowing ski pants, I go up on a chairlift – up the two thousand feet to the top. Blessed to be in a rocking chair with two thousand feet of snow and precipice under my dangling feet. 'This is the day the Lord has made: let us rejoice and be glad in it.'

That night the storyteller and Deputy Minister of Environment, Paul Dean, kindly gives me a lift back up to the airport at Deer Lake. In the dark the first rains of the year are falling and we hit nine flash floods on the highway. Spring approacheth.

The eighteen-seater plane *en route* from Goose Bay in Labrador stops to pick us up and fly us on to St John's. Near St John's the turbulence is so naked that even the oil-rig man beside me is blushing but again the pilot brings us down immaculately. Just in the nick of time for me to catch the midnight Air Canada flight back to London.

Back in Dublin the following day at noon I return, with my heart sinking down into my guts, to my black cave. 'I found Dublin people cold and angry,' a friendly Newfoundlander confided in me. But I lift up my soul by recalling the latest news in Newfoundland. Reuters News Agency has learned that there was a small house-fire in the White House a few weeks ago in which the President's entire personal library was burnt – all two volumes of it. To make matters worse, President Bush had not finished colouring in the second volume.

March 19, 2003

NEWFOUNDLAND 2

'All dem bombs with de darlin' names: Tomahawk, Cruise, Microwave, Smartie. Every night LIVE on de telly from Baghdad! Operation "Shock and Awe"! Darlin' Nazi terminogoly! Shock UND Awe! Oh it's a darlin' blitzkrieg, Captain Bertie, a darlin' blitzkrieg!'

'Oh for de love of de Dubs, Joxer, will ye desist.'

On the morning of Tuesday November 14, 2000, at 11 a.m. in the bar of Jury's Hotel in Ballsbridge, I met with Al Pittman who – but alas in my provincial ignorance I did not know at the time – was the Patrick Kavanagh of modern Newfoundland literature. A warm, affectionate, nervous man, he told me all about the festival that he and his friend Rex Brown had started in Corner Brook, Newfoundland fourteen years earlier. A celebration of music and poetry, a *gathering*, he said, of friends old and new and they called it The March Hare. He invited me to attend. Alas, Al Pittman died nine months later on August 26, 2001 aged sixty-one years.

However, Al's bosom friend and co-founder of The March

Hare, Rex Brown, renewed the invitation and that's how in this March of 2003 I came to be in Newfoundland to give poetry recitals at The Sixteenth Annual March Hare gathering in St John's, Gander and Corner Brook.

This year's March Hare started with the launch on Ash Wednesday afternoon, in The Ship Inn in St John's, of an anthology of contemporary Newfoundland and Labrador and Irish poetry compiled by John Ennis of the Waterford Institute of Technology and Stephanie McKenzie of Memorial University at Corner Brook. Entitled *The Backyards of Heaven*, this massive 350-page anthology represents almost every Newfoundland and Labrador poet and almost every Irish poet. The book – only €15 – will be launched on this side of the North Atlantic tomorrow week, Thursday April 3, at 5 p.m. in Oscar's Restaurant in the Waterford I.T. with six poets from Newfoundland: Randall Maggs, Michael Crummey, Mary Dalton, Chief Misel Joe, Kyran Pittman and Johnny Burton. Again in Cork at 7 p.m. in the Metropole on April 4; Galway at the Atlanta, 6 p.m. on April 5; Dublin, April 6 at the Writers Centre, 6 p.m.; and April 7 in Belfast at the Linenhall, 5 p.m. Refreshments and music and – admission *free*!

The March Hare proper began on the night of Ash Wednesday in the Masonic Temple in St John's. 'Are you going for the Handshake?' a local man asked John Ennis. Among glass cases of the tools of Masonry – gavels, hammers, spatulas – we listened to Al Pittman's comrade, the poet Enos Watts, whispering his laconic incantations and to Stephanie and Daniel Payne singing, in their glacial sunlight voices, old songs and new songs by Stephanie herself – as mesmerising a young singer as the young Joan Baez. I heard Mary Dalton, Newfoundland's first woman poet, reading her 'merrybegot', meaning 'lovechild'. Merrybegot!

In Corner Brook in a downtown bar, Casual Jacks – the equivalent of McDaids and O'Donoghues as they were forty years ago, not the trendy, unrecognisable drinkeries of Dublin 2003 – I heard a night of song, music, poetry and storytelling.

Casual Jack's was Al Pittman's bar; he always sat at the counter in the same corner, a rum and coke to hand. A Newfoundland Hemingway/Kerouac but his own man who never gave an inch to the politics of poetry or to the politics of fame. An outstanding athlete and fisherman as well as the first modern poet of Newfoundland.

I heard the Deputy Minister of Environment in the Government of Newfoundland and Labrador, Paul Dean from Placentia Bay, read his own Christmas story entitled 'Come On With The Punt'; as vivid a tale as Dylan Thomas's 'A Child's Christmas in Wales'. I heard thirty-year-old Lisa Moore from Portugal Cove read from her best-selling book of short stories called *Open*. Wow! A fresh new voice with a vengeance. Lisa Moore is one of a movement of writers known as The Burning Rock. I heard Pamela Morgan from Grand Falls sing her own song 'Stealer of Hearts'.

The next night in Corner Brook – 'Pittman's Fancy' – The March Hare moved across the street to the Columbus Club, the H.Q. of the Knights of Columbanus. High on a wall of the vast function room, tiny portraits of Christopher Columbus, John Paul II and Queen Elizabeth II.

I heard young local man Michael Winter read from his cool new novel called *This all Happened*. I heard Anita Best sing cross-handed. I heard Ken Jacobsen in the voice of Johnny Cash sing a song called 'A Boy Named George': 'My name's Dubya, how does that rub ya.'

One of the sponsors of the new anthology is the Ireland Newfoundland Partnership (the INP) and thereby – in these nightmare nights of Reichsführer Rumsfeld and Reichsmarshal Perle (the American Reich's reign of terror in Iraq where children constitute more than fifty per cent of the population) – hangs a happy tale.

In 1976 John Bruton, aged twenty-nine, went on holiday to Newfoundland. He knew the saga of the pre-famine migrations in the eighteenth and nineteenth centuries from Waterford, Wexford, Cork and Tipperary to south-east Newfoundland. In 1976, a handsome curly-headed bachelor as well as parliamentary secretary to the Minister of Industry and Commerce, he found himself – aided and abetted by former RTÉ broadcaster Aidan O'Hara – at house-parties on the Irish Shore and was amazed at the Irishness of it all. He became fascinated by how the Irish way of life has remained intact but not fossilised in Newfoundland. In 1996 John Bruton as Taoiseach returned to Newfoundland on a state visit and struck up a friendship with their Premier, Brian Tobin, and the two countries negotiated a Memorandum of Understanding out of which was born in 2001 a governmental business agency named the Ireland Newfoundland Partnership with an office in the Department of Enterprise, Trade and Employment and a full-time director, Agnes Aylward, a rotating staff of Newfoundland post-graduates and a Board under the Chairmanship of Michael Ahern, TD, Minister of State for Trade and Commerce. The Partnership is concerned to facilitate political, economic and cultural links between the two countries and, by God, but we do have so much in common. I dare say no two countries in the world have so much in common as Ireland and Newfoundland: marine exploration, aquaculture and fishing, offshore oil and gas, ecology-based tourism, music, poetry and storytelling, symbiotic relationships with bullyboy neighbours.

Many more Newfoundlanders visit Ireland than vice versa. But the Partnership is set to change all that and already in the Waterford Institute of Technology Dr John Ennis has set up a Centre for Newfoundland and Labrador Studies.

Half the population of Newfoundland is Irish, living mostly in thriving urban centres whilst their coastal communities struggle for survival. The landscape is Irish. When President McAleese visited in October 1998 she moved tough-skinned Newfoundlanders to tears when she said: 'Now I understand why the Irish came here – I recognise the landscape.' Tourism in Newfoundland is as important to them as it to us, but they have the same problems as we do, including the dilemmas of how to reach your market and how to manage a prosperous ecology-based tourism without harming the environment and losing your soul.

Our common heritage poses fascinating questions. How is it that the Irish way of life is more intact in Newfoundland than it is here in Ireland? How is it that language is more alive over there? Three weeks ago in St John's, the oldest city in Canada, Agnes Aylward heard Ally O'Brien, a sixth-generation eighty-seven-year-old Irish Newfoundlander, sing 'Ban Cnoic Éireann Ó' while outside in the snow his ninety-year-old brother was turning his tractor. How is it that Newfoundlanders are friendlier than we are in their cities and towns where random violence is unknown? Is it neighbourhood living? Friendly neighbours?

'How or never, it's back now to de darlin' newspaper headlines: "Baghdad's Night of Terror", "War Without Mercy", "Mass Destruction". Darlin' blitzkrieg, Captain Bertie, darlin' blitzkrieg!

March 26, 2003

THE INVASION OF IRAQ

Twenty years ago, in late February 1983, I made my first visit to the Soviet Union: Moscow, Leningrad, Armenia, Estonia. Born in 1944 I had been reared by Church and State here in Ireland to fear all Communists, especially Soviet Communists, as evil people with cloven hooves, even more sinister than Protestants. I was shocked to meet Russian communists who were kindly, decent, hardworking, playful, spiritual people, as well as hard-hearted, stony-faced men and women; the worst I met was a glamorous, middle-aged woman who at a formal committee meeting castigated me for my sympathetic remarks concerning the poet Pasternak, author of *Dr Zhivago*. As for the Kremlin old boys, they were a replica of the Maynooth Hierarchy: Cardinal Chernenko strutting about Maynooth with the grimmer-faced Archbishop Andropov.

At the end of that first visit, I felt grief-stricken at saying goodbye not only to some salt-of-the-earth individuals but also to the masses of peoples I'd seen on the streets and trains and in the cemeteries of the twenty million dead of the Second World War. These anonymous Russian faces changed my way of looking at history and evolution. I realised that war was no longer an option. As of now – the late twentieth century, the beginning of the twenty-first – in a crisis, be it personal, societal, national, international, war is no longer on the evolutionary menu. If man persists on the path of war, then the evolution of the human species has come to an end.

On arriving back in London, early March 1983, the newspaper headlines were proclaiming President Reagan's speech in Orlando, Florida in which he branded Russia as 'the *focus* of evil in the modern world'. This sophisticated analysis was to be refined by George W. Bush as 'the *axis* of evil in the modern world'. It was on that grey March day in 1983 that the dime finally dropped in my soul and I realised for the first time the enormity of the tragedy of the modern world; that in fact the human species was doomed unless small, independent nations like Ireland and the countries of the old world, of Europe and Asia, could bring Washington to its senses.

I realised that President Reagan first of all was choosing the path of war and, second, he was, although he did not know it, referring to his own US administration. Like most Irishmen and Irishwomen I cherish America and features of the American way of life; it was traumatic to have to accept that the cancer that was destroying the human species was located in Washington and that sooner or later it would destroy not only America itself but the entire human species.

Studying the pathology of the American cancer, one asks: how and when did it start? No one knows for sure but it was probably on August 6, 1945 when the US dropped the atom bomb on Hiroshima. I suspected as much all my life but after visiting Hiroshima in 1998 I became almost certain. The rot became melodramatically visible during the presidency of the smarmy liar Richard Nixon and his grotesquely comic sidekick Dr Kissinger, who it was hard not to think was Dame Peter Sellers in disguise. President Jimmy Carter offered a glimpse of redemption, but his frail candle was snuffed out by Ronald Reagan who gave the disease a sort of macabre panache. His sister patient, of course, was Margaret Thatcher who roamed the world in search of war from the Falklands to Northern Ireland and who so eloquently defined the Thatcher-Reagan era when she said: 'There is no such thing as society.'

Among President Reagan's most destructive achievements was his invention and manipulation of the Soviet Communist leader M. S. Gorbachev. Overnight in the mid-eighties Gorbachev was assembled and packaged for American and British consumption in the certain knowledge that anything other than gradual reforms of the Soviet Union would result in disaster for many of the countries that comprised the Soviet Union and, most of all, Russia itself. Just as in recent weeks during the blitzkrieg of Baghdad, American and British corporations have been squabbling for lucrative contracts to rebuild Iraq after Bush has destroyed it, so Reagan, behind the smokescreen of the hapless Gorbachev, cleared the way for American and Western business and finance to invade Russia and make a quick buck. That this resulted in the disintegration of Russian society delighted Reagan and Thatcher.

During the 1990s – the Clinton years – again there flickered possibilities of hope that the final holocaust might be avoided. Clinton was loathed by Cheney, Rumsfeld and the Bush family for many reasons, chief among them his efforts to bring even a little justice and sense to foreign policy. But by the year 2000, the year of Dubya's election, the American empire, having devoured and spat out the Soviet Union, was like an itchy dinosaur scanning the globe for another lump of the world to destroy. 'IRAQ' – whooped

Dubya. And so he began his crusade against Iraq only to be halted in his tracks by the Hollywood blockbuster of 9/11.

9/11 was a godsend to President Bush. The Iraq war was put on hold and instead the entire Muslim world from North Africa to the Middle East to the Far East became the target. And so we had the devastation of Afghanistan. But then what? Back to Iraq where we are now engulfed in carnage which, although horrendous, is providing mass entertainment to the home audience of Fox TV and other networks. Only the lone, brave voices of our own Richard Downes in Baghdad and Channel 4's Lindsey Hilsum, the *Irish Independent's* Robert Fisk and *The Irish Times*' Lara Marlowe give us clues to the truth of what is really happening. And yet, before the invasion began, we saw Cheney on March 16 on Channel 4 confide to us: 'The Iraqis want us to liberate them,' and on March 12, again on Channel 4, Richard Perle had told us: 'The Iraqis will not die for Saddam; there will be no resistance.'

Last year on August 14 the aged American Jesuit priest Fr Daniel Berrigan spoke gently, quietly and briefly to a massive, spilling-out-on-the-streets audience in the Tony O'Reilly Hall in Great Denmark Street, Dublin 1. Referring to the looming American invasion of Iraq, Fr Berrigan observed that the whole immediate nightmare revolved around what he called 'the festering wound of Israel and Palestine'.

In March 1993 in Jerusalem I was asked by Israeli State TV to make a ten-minute film for their Friday-night politics programme, their equivalent of our *Prime Time*. During the filming of that piece, I walked through the alleyways of the Old City speaking to the few Palestinian men who were standing about at street corners – the first *intifada* was still ongoing – and later talking to a middle-aged Russian Jew singing for his supper in Ben Yehuda Street, the Grafton Street of modern Jerusalem. I was followed by the cameraman and sound crew and, at a distance of about forty yards, two young men in jeans and trainers dodging discreetly in and out of sight with machine-guns hidden in their rucksacks. To camera I talked about what I felt about terror, both Israeli state terror and Palestinian terror. I talked about war and where it was leading the human species.

After the programme was transmitted a Palestinian writer denounced me as a stooge of the Israeli regime but he did not impress me because he struck me as a hockey mistress – just like Rumsfeld strikes me as a hockey mistress. In fact, the film crew I had worked with opened my eyes to the tragedy at the heart of Israel and Palestine: the civil war between secular Jews and orthodox Jews. By the end of the 1990s the orthodox Jews, having assassinated Rabin, had won their civil war and, backed to the hilt by President Bush, the great contemporary secular Jewish activists such as the former Deputy Mayor of Jerusalem, Meron Benvenisti, have been vanquished.

From a Muslim point of view one of the queerest things about the American Empire is its claim to be Christian. You do not have to be a theologian to see that the American Empire is a parody, a contradiction, of Christian ethics and, as I speak, President Bush is hell-bent on the crucifixion of the human family – of the child, the mother and the father. The biblical words from last Saturday's Mass repudiate Emperor Bush:

> *What I want is love, not sacrifice;*
> *knowledge of God, not holocausts.*

April 2, 2003

SHEILA MACBRIDE

I drive out to the outskirts of Baghdad to visit my mother, Sheila MacBride, in the nursing home in which she has been sailing out into the middle of the Arabian Sea of Alzheimer's for the last eighteen months. As I drive across the Tigris I watch another American bomb blacken, then redden the sky ahead of me. As Richard Downes coolly observed last week 'It's getting hard to know the difference here between day and night.' How the laptop generals would love to incinerate an Alzheimer's nursing home and then claim it was a stash of weapons of mass destruction. What great fun it is to be an old woman in an Alzheimer's nursing home whilst the Great Teacher from Texas is teaching you 'Shock and Awe'.

I climb up the silent staircase, negotiating the bolted gate and the locked door.

At the door of her ward – or, I should say, nursery, for an Alzheimer's nursing home is a crèche for the aged, with lots of teddy bears and baby dolls strewn about – at the door I glimpse Mummy. She is over near the window in her day clothes but lying up on a chair-bed with her frail feet swathed. From across the vast desert of the tiny ward she gives me that old quizzical look. Then, that old smile of hers with its sandstorm of mother-son implications. The smile increases. I begin my approach. The kindly nurse cries: 'Look who's here to see you!' Mummy, maintaining her quizzical smile, says: 'Again?' In spite of all the automatic gunfire raking through her skull, splattering all the world with the bloody grey matter of her brains, Mummy can still make a joke, can still laugh, can still smile. She always had the keenest sense of the black joke of life. Neither the bloodthirsty larceny of Iraq's oil fields nor the usurpation of Irish soil for a war summit in the name of peace would surprise her.

It is two o'clock in the afternoon and Mummy is wide awake in the company of her sister patients who are asleep sitting-up under notices on the wall which say: 'Hoist Only When Necessary'; 'Inflate Only When Necessary'. Mummy can scarcely speak anymore. When she tries to speak, she cannot finish the sentence. An entire thought occurs to her but by the time she gets half-way through her sentence, the second half has disappeared from her screen. She is excited by my new shirt – a large red and black plaid shirt which I purchased in Newfoundland – but she can speak only through her eyes. She is amused by the sight of me in a plaid shirt and white trainers, as much as to say, and laugh at the same time: son, will you never grow up? I compliment her on her wine-red cardigan and white blouse.

Amazing her good form considering the pain she is in. Her lovely hands are almost paralysed by osteoporosis and arthritis.

I sit down opposite Mummy and after a pensive interval she resumes smiling quizzically at me. I smile back. And so we commune. Mummy, you and I, two hurt hawks eyeing one another in afternoon sunlight. My head throbbing with the puking of cluster bombs, your head shell-shocked with another but no less awful and shocking blitzkrieg. But even if you did know about the violation of the laws of the United Nations and of God by Bush and Blair it would only confirm your lifelong view of the world of men as a pretty bad world. When you yourself were five years old the Black and Tans came to your home in Mayo and took away your father as a hostage and you clung to your mother's skirts screaming and weeping. Later it was de Valera's men who took him away again and, when finally he returned home, he remained mostly silent for the rest of his days – fifteen years of mostly silent days. Almost as silent as you are now, and it near broke your mother's heart as well as your own heart too. So that you never spoke of your father down your own eighty-seven years. Only when Professor Alois Alzheimer rang the bell of the door to the sarcophagus of your lonely apartment did you begin to recall and talk urgently about your father, Joseph MacBride.

So many things you were silent about, Mummy. The poet William Yeats who caused your family, the MacBrides, such grief. Funny that one of his most beautiful poems, 'The Gift of Harun Al-Raschid', not only was set in Baghdad but, as in so much of his greatest poetry, was a celebration of war. Our national poet was a glorifier of war.

No sound in the room except for our own breathing and the sighs and snores of sleeping ladies and the transistor radio on the chest of drawers out of which I can hear the ack-ack-ack of hysterical voices. Outside the window the sky is black with smoke and orange with fire. You smile. In the landscape of Alzheimer's, Bush and Blair are, to borrow a typical expression of yours, 'par for the course'. Two war-driven men surrounded by cliques of male addicts of power and the odd female. Out of your eighty-seven years of suffering in this life you gaze at me like a seventeenth-century headstone with an indecipherable inscription, sunken in long grass, all skull and bone.

In the droning silence, I try to say prayers, mutely. Mummy gazes upwards towards the sun in the tall window overlooking the Sugar Loaf. Suddenly I remember I have a paperback volume of the Psalms in my bag. The Psalms: those rubies of Arabian culture. I fish it out. I read aloud Psalm 41 – the Psalm in this morning's Mass:

> *Like the deer that yearns*
> *For running streams,*
> *So my soul is yearning*
> *For you, my God.*

Immediately Mummy attempts to sit up. I have not seen her attempt to sit upright for nearly a year. She strives to read the words as I speak them and I hold the book close up to her face. I search for another favourite psalm of my own but I cannot find it – the one about the returned exile:

> *They go out, they go out full of tears*
> *Carrying seed for the sowing:*
> *They come back, they come back, full of song,*
> *Carrying their sheaves.*

Instead I read Psalm 102. The kindly nurse has woken up one of the other ladies to cut her fingernails. To the music of the nail scissors I read out Psalm 102:

> *The Lord is compassion and love,*
> *Slow to anger and rich in mercy.*
> *His wrath will come to an end;*
> *He will not be angry for ever …*

They shoot journalists, don't they?

> *By the waters of Babylon*
> *There we sat down;*
> *Yea, we wept,*
> *When we remembered Zion.*

Time to leave and drive back to my cave in Ringsend. In the doorway of the ward, I stand and wave and wave and wave. Mummy struggles to lift a crippled hand but it won't unlock for her. Instead, she beams, a lighthouse in the fog. I want to weep; I want to scream. O dearest mother, brave, brave, after a hard unrewarding life, marooned at the end of your precious life's trek across the Arabian wastes. My God, my God, O why have we abandoned thee?

Driving back across the Tigris I continue my conversation with Mummy, thinking of Daddy too who died from television-watching and how we used love going on picnics before the war, especially to Ur. Mummy, do you remember Ur? Ur of the Chaldees? I'm sure you do, only you're not telling anyone anymore. A pair of old Baghdadis are we, Mummy, old Babylonians, Ur folk, and we'll stay in Baghdad, we'll stay in Babylon, we'll stay in Ur. In the Mass this morning Nebuchadnezzar gets a roasting but he's *our* Nebuchadnezzar – *our* Nebuchadnezzar of Babylon. Let Bush & Blair PLC bomb Baghdad and Babylon and Ur until they're blue in their faces, we'll not budge from Baghdad, we'll not budge from Babylon, we'll not budge from Ur. Baghdad and Babylon and Ur is where we come from and, by God, Mummy, Baghdad and Babylon and Ur is where we'll stay.

The Lord is close to the broken-hearted

April 9, 2003

Street Life

We are most of us hypocrites and I am no less of a hypocrite than anyone else.

My hypocrisy comes into its own and shines forth when I am confronted by the spectacle of another human being begging on the street. My conscience starts hopping up and down in its box, wriggling this way and that way, trying to satisfy its own craving for justification.

I am scurrying along Nassau Street or Stephen's Green or Baggot Street. At a distance of twenty to thirty yards I can see the body of a young man seated on the pavement against a wall with his head bowed and an empty cup in his hands. Conscience cringes, snivelling: 'You can make your contribution on your way back after you've done your messages.' Conscience, with its repertoire of self-deception, often wins out and the slave in me submits and I walk past briskly, keeping to the kerb and giving my fellow human being on the pavement a wide berth and subsequently succeeding in forgetting all about him. Funny how each of us has our own style of giving a destitute body a wide berth; we could measure ourselves by the different styles of our meanness.

Luckily, however, I have a soul as well as a conscience and, immediately conscience gets up to its mean, devious tricks, my soul awakens from its torpor and wrestles to get the better of conscience and, when it does, I put my hand in my pocket and drop a coin or coins into the empty cup, at the same time saying to the young man: 'Are you sleeping out these days?' 'Yes,' he replies and I enquire where and he describes to me a particular shop doorway that he favours. A hostel – he explains to me – is too expensive and, besides, there is a queue and, even if has enough money for one night, there will probably be no bed available. His dream, he tells me, is a long-stay bed in the Iveagh Hostel but the chances of that are almost nil. He – or she – is *not* on drink or drugs, which of course proves a major disappointment to any virtuous citizen to whom I may happen to report my encounter.

So why is he on the streets? Actually that's none of my business but he tells me anyway. His mother has taken up with a new man and the new man who is a bowsy has turfed him out of the flat.

I wish him 'Good luck' and continue on my way, filthy conscience trying to hint that I have done a good deed but my soul making it crystal clear that I have done nothing of the sort. My financial contribution has been miserable and it is always miserable; so totally out of proportion that it exposes me not only as a hypocrite but as a ludicrous hypocrite. Conscience retorts by claiming that almost everyone else also is a ludicrous hypocrite. True but irrelevant. What counts is my own ludicrosity, not anyone else's ludicrosity; my own hypocrisy, not your hypocrisy.

A Romanian woman stops me in my tracks and pleads for money for her child and herself. Again conscience rears its disgusting puss and screeches: 'Look at her beautiful clothes, look at how contentedly her baby sleeps in her arms.' But again, if I'm lucky, my soul will come to my rescue and remind me that it is none of my business how beautiful her skirts and shawls are nor how contentedly her baby sleeps; the only relevant fact being that no human being on this planet will beg on the streets except in dire circumstances of misfortune. Don't you know that by now, Durcan? You who in your youth had to beg and scrounge and shift on the streets of alien cities and knock on strange doors at night in search of a bed? Except for jail, it is the first and last humiliation: to be compelled by circumstance to beg on the streets.

Ginger in my soul reveals to me that the human being who is doing the begging nearly always gives more to the wretched donor than the wretched donor gives to the indigent one. The middle-aged man playing the banjo thanks me for my miserable contribution and says: 'Actually I can't play the banjo, as you can probably see and hear, but I feel I ought to be doing something, do you know what I mean?' He tells me he lives in Coolock but he gets the bus into town most days to play the banjo.

Conscience persists with its lies, trying to suggest that the human being begging in the street is somehow inferior to the upstanding passers-by. Only my soul is capable of telling the truth, which is that, in the face of the certain mortality of every single one of us, no human being is superior to any other human being. Can you hear me, President Bush? The children whom your marines terrorised and shot before our eyes on the streets of Baghdad are as important as you, sir, which is why I for one cannot look at your photograph without feeling sick.

And yet in Ireland probably at least one-third of our population is so well off as to make themselves look even more ludicrous than I look myself. One third of the population is so well off that for them 'problems' are problems of luxury. 'Antigone, dear – I do like your new formica table top on the patio – do you think I should really change my car? Last thing Sophocles says to me every night is: what you need, puss-in-boots, is a change of car. But, Antigone dear, I have to say to Sophocles – poor Sophocles up to his neck in tribunals – I am so busy arranging our next vacation in Dubai that I haven't time even to think about changing my car. In fact, if I was to tell you God's own truth, Antigone, it's not the next vacation but the next vacation after the next vacation that has me frazzled. Sophocles wants us to go to Fiji for Christmas.'

And yet Lent – only four days to go now before the end of Lent – Lent has, as one of its original, long-lost purposes, the practice of alms-giving on a serious level, that is to say on a scale beyond our normal hypocrisy levels.

But here in Ireland for all of my lifetime, since 1944, not only the well-off but many of the bishops and archbishops of the Roman Catholic Church demeaned Lent just as they demeaned most all else in our lives. The grim grey men turned Lent into a black, life-denying season in which they fostered melancholia whilst they cosied their coffers, thereby rendering the word 'Lent' a word synonymous with negativity. In fact the word 'Lent' is one of the most beautiful words in the English language. Lent! Meaning 'springtime'. From the Old English.

So, come out your soul now in these last days of Lent, come leaping and budding and flowering along the streets, filling empty cups and beakers and caps and hats to overflowing so that on Easter Sunday morning Christ truly may rise from the dead and the sun dance three times on the rooftops.

And yet how strange a thing it is to say but after sixteen or seventeen hundred years of Christianity in Ireland, Christ's mercy and compassion seem to have vanished from our social and political life just as they seem to have vanished from social and political life in the western world at large. Indeed, to the almighty war leaders Bush and Blair, the entire Arab world seems to be regarded by them as a world of street beggars whom the West has decided to wage world war on. When the Easter Candle is lit on this Easter Sunday, we should seriously ask ourselves if, in our indifference to destitution on our own streets and in our war on the Arab world, we have any right to light such a candle in the name of Christ, Jesus the Palestinian pacifist, the eccentric vagrant, the radical idealist, the itinerant beggar.

April 16, 2003

Rosie Walking

My granddaughter Rosie – Rosie Joyce aged one year and ten months – takes me for a three-hour walk in the Botanic Gardens. It is my first voyage with her since, abruptly, she started walking a month ago.

She starts off our space-walk by flinging herself down on the bronze plaque set in the pavement and with her miniscule fingers traces the words for me: a quotation from Lucretius, the first-century BC Roman poet: 'This dread and darkness of the mind cannot be dispelled by the sunbeams, the shining shafts of day but only by an understanding of the outward forms and inner workings of nature.' Rosie swims to her feet as delicately as an astronaut and takes off at a sidelong totter uphill and I have to zoom after her. For the rest of the afternoon she continues to put the heart across me as she canters on, full of horse, full of galaxies, full of innocence cascading forth its snow like the magnolias up in the magnolia garden enclosed behind the wrought-iron trellises of clematis. Every time noise starts up in the sky she halts and, pointing upwards, cries: 'Plane! Plane!' I close my eyes. The airplane is mankind's most exquisite invention but, by the same token, dropping bombs out of airplanes is the zenith of human depravity.

Rosie trundles on and on but not of course in a straight line. A small tubby Buddha in orange anorak, blue pants rolled half-way up her shins, red socks, brand-new red shoes, she tilts from side to side and topples around in circles and stops and stands and ponders all that is around her. Everything and everybody engrosses her. She stops and stares at people and they stop and smile at her and, as they pass by, she waves each of them goodbye. At every flowerbed she sits down on the edge, her front-row seat, and, pointing at the flowers, explains them to me: 'Flowers! Flowers!' She bounces along ahead of me and disappears into the rhododendron glasshouse. I follow her in and underneath the counters of pots she points at the beds of gravel and cries out 'Gravel! Gravel!' We turn a corner and come upon an indoor waterfall. Rosie kneels down on the floor, resting her elbows on the ledge of the waterfall and cries out 'Water! Water!' Ten minutes later she is still kneeling at this newfound altar of magic – a waterfall! And I think of the Arab tribesman whom Saint-Euxpéry invited to visit him in France and how he knelt in wonder when Saint-Euxpéry took him to see a natural waterfall and how, when Saint-Euxpéry said it was time to leave, the Arab tribesman exclaimed 'But may we not wait until they switch off the waterfall?'

And, as Rosie kneels under me in the same state of grace and wonder, I think of the people of Iraq of whom more than fifty per cent are children under the age of fifteen and of the drinking water fouled by the American Air Force and of the terror they have been subjected to in what the Americans boast of as the most shocking blitzkrieg in all of history. And I think also of their parents and grandparents all of whom are children of God as they are children also in the sense that that

Arab tribesman contemplating the natural waterfall in France was a child. In war-freaks like Rumsfeld, Perle and Wolfowitz, the child has long since died which makes them the terrifying killing machines that they are; ex-children who have broken the laws of God as well as the laws of the United Nations and the Geneva Convention.

Rosie, Rosie, how you could teach them if they would only watch you. But they are long past contemplating anything except their own world empire, perhaps the final empire of human history.

Out of the rhododendron glasshouse and up the hill of fir trees and into the oak garden.

I lie down in the grass and stretch out but Rosie stays standing, looking, looking, looking, contemplating, contemplating, contemplating. She gazes up into the treetops and it dawns on me that she is trying to locate the source of the birdsong. She picks up an oak leaf from last autumn and analyses its hard, brown texture before finally, like the priest breaking the bread of the Eucharist, she breaks the leaf and holds it out to me. I offer her a daisy.

We resume our road and Rosie barrels up the tar macadam to a bench. She has a penchant for benches. I sit her up on the green boards of the bench and she cries 'Drink, drink.' From my bag I produce her milk-beaker and she swallows long and deep before gasping 'Aaaaah.' She cries 'Biccie, biccie.' Desultorily munching on a biccie, she is content to survey the passing scene for a quarter of an hour.

In a clump of trees stands a dark bush, President Bush, with his arms hanging out by his sides like a country-and-western ape. Why in these last minutes of evolution – in the injury-time of evolution – does President Bush insist on his country-and-western ape posture? He terrifies me but Rosie takes no notice of his antics. Stupid ape!

Back down on her feet she totters on at full throttle. We meet other omniscient Under Twos. Oscar Lambe, who introduces me to his mother Lynette. Kathleen, who is only fourteen months but can already stand, with her Czech parents from near the Austrian border. We facilitate a young man from Latvia, who is photographing his girlfriend, by taking a photograph of them as a couple with their digital camera. Rosie cries 'Camera! Camera!'

By the gossiping waters of the River Tolka stands a statue of Socrates in his bare feet and white cloak. Rosie fondles his toes and his shins. She waves: 'Bye-bye Socrates.'

Another green bench. This time Rosie wants to use it as a table to lean on and slap. She scrutinises its rivets. After a session of swinging out of it and slapping up against it, Rosie wants to stand on it and use it as a tightrope to frighten the daylights out of me. Up and down she wobbles, three feet off the ground.

Away again along the path, swaying, stumbling, careening, bumping but never, not once even, falling. Halting, she addresses me imperiously: 'Tissue.' She gives two elderly ladies a demonstration, crying out: 'Tissue, tissue.' One of the ladies compliments her: 'Good girl.' Rosie looks her straight in the eye and compliments her back: 'Good girl.'

The three hours have flown past and her energy is at the same pitch as it was when we started out. But I have orders from her Daddy to have her home for 5 p.m. teatime. Outside her terrace house she lifts the flap of the letter-box, raises herself up on tippy-toes and cries 'Daddy, Daddy.'

In the kitchen, after lashing down a bowl of chicken and sesame seeds, she introduces me to a soft-toy black cat with yellow spots and she cries out 'Cheet-ah! Cheet-ah!' Next a teddy bear called 'Norwich'. She cries 'Teddy! Teddy!' Next she hands me a large public-library book and slaps me on the knee. I hop her up and she goes into what I call Rosie-Spasm as she always does when being read to and at other classified moments of take-off. I read to her a strange Russian tale about Trublov the mouse who wants to learn how to play the balalaika. Every time I utter the word 'balalaika' Rosie goes into Rosie-Spasm, kicking out her feet, opening her mouth wide as she can, shuddering all over, all rockets firing. Outer Space!

Time for me to go. Bye, Rosie, bye. In her mother my daughter Sarah's arms tiny Rosie bunches up her eyes and, laughing with her teeth shut tight, she waves. I drive across Baghdad to my cave in Ringsend. Dodging small-arms fire, I make a dash from car to cave and lying down on my bed I listen to the hi-fi of precision bombing and I weep dry tears. If only the Whacker Bush wanted to learn the balalaika. But he wouldn't even know what a balalaika is. O Rosie, God help us!

April 23, 2003

OSAMA BIN BUSH

During the anarchy that accompanied the occupation of Baghdad, when I bumped into a friend and I referred to the war he stopped me: 'Paul, I have two children aged twelve and ten and when the invasion started I decided I wanted no part of it in my life and home.' A man protecting his family from military pornography.

But I live alone and when the invasion of Iraq started on March 20, this day seven weeks ago, I decided to witness as best I could. For the three weeks of blitzkrieg, and for the four weeks of anarchy that have followed, every evening I have watched the *Six-One* news on RTÉ 1 to see Richard Downes live from Baghdad and Channel 4 news to see Lindsey Hilsum. I have kept a twenty-four-hour watch on Sky and BBC for breaking news. Every morning I have read Lara Marlowe in *The Irish Times* and Robert Fisk in *The Independent*. I have consulted magazines including *The New Yorker*, the current issue of which carries a corpse-by-innocent-corpse report by Jon Lee Anderson and his account of American etiquette in Baghdad: 'A Marine officer was reading a copy of *Playboy* as he defecated into a milk crate. He waved when we passed.'

I am startled by the barbarity practised by the American regime – heirs of the great civilising documents of the Declaration of Independence and the American Constitution – and I am only now becoming aware that it proposes itself to the world as an American version of al Qaeda. This is the self-styled 'Project for the New American Century' faction, and Bush is the front man. Their ideology is terror from the top down, in contrast to al Qaeda which instigates terror from the base up. 'The Project for the New American Century' faction proposes a World War IV in which America takes over the entire world. So it is that we find ourselves living in the era of Osama Bin Bush. France is about to be punished for opposing the war. What would have happened to Ireland if we had withdrawn landing rights at Shannon? Mr Ahern would have got more than a kick up the G.P.O. The Project was started many years before 9/11 by a faction about whom not much is known by the outside world, and very little by the American populace. The central players are Douglas Feith, Scooter Libby, John R. Bolton, Elliot Abrams, Paul 'Wolfie' Wolfowitz, Donald 'Rummy' Rumsfeld, Dick Cheney, James Woolsey, William Kristol, Richard Perle, Jay Garner, Rupert Murdoch, Conrad Black and former RTÉ correspondent and speech writer for Mrs Thatcher and chief of the UPI news agency John O'Sullivan. This tiny faction has hi-jacked American foreign policy.

Consider the destruction in Baghdad of the National Museum and the burning of the National Library and the Islamic Library. Before the invasion, American and British museum curators and librarians pleaded with the Pentagon not to jeopardise the archives of the ten-thousand-year-old Iraqi civilisation. The Pentagon insisted that the museums and libraries would be safeguarded but, whilst they protected the Oil Ministry, they ignored the destruction of the archives of not only Iraqi but world civilisation 'on a scale', wrote the conservative Alexander Chancellor in last Saturday's *Guardian*, 'without parallel in modern times and unequalled in Iraq since the Mongol invasion of Baghdad in 1258'.

Saddam Hussein is a brutal leader in the classic barbarian mould but so also is Donald Rumsfeld. On April 16 he organised a Country and Western victory gig in the Pentagon. In *The Irish Times* of April 5 Conor O'Clery reported that Rumsfeld enjoys quoting Al Capone: 'You'll get more with a kind word and a gun than a kind word alone.'

The same Rumsfeld who delights to pontificate on the torture chambers of Saddam Hussein refuses angrily to comment on his own torture chambers at Guantanamo Bay.

I have been startled also by the brazen mendacity practiced day in, day out by the invaders. In the Azores three days before the blitzkrieg, President Bush threw a piece of bait to the Arab world which he called 'The Road Map to Peace'. This would accomplish, he told us, an independent Palestinian State by 2005. What a whopper! What a black, black joke!

That is what is new in the American invasion; the black comedy of it all culminating, on the one hand, on April 14 in the liberation of one of Baghdad's largest mental hospitals and the spectacle of six hundred mental patients roaming the streets whilst in general hospitals doctors doubled as grave-diggers and, on the other hand, the Big Tent Meeting on April 15 at Ur in Babylon at which the pro-Israeli American sixty-five-year-old arms dealer appointed by Bush to govern Iraq, General Jay Garner, rhapsodised to a rent-a-crowd of Iraqis about how wonderful it was to wake up that morning in Ur the birthplace of Abraham. 'Missile contractor' is the Pentagon-preferred designation of General Garner. In *The Irish Times* last Friday Lisa Marlowe quoted General Garner: 'We fought probably the most merciful war in the history of warfare.' Four weeks ago today Marlowe reported '33 civilians die in Babylon bombing.' Under her report, a photograph of an Iraqi man, his arms raised to heaven, wailing over the carcasses of his three precision-bombed children.

The glossary of war has been perfected by the Americans: hammer time; shock and awe; collateral damage; A-Day; throwing in the whole package; Operation Iraqi Freedom; surgical strike; psychops; to neutralise; to take out; to decapitate; to war game; body bags; freedom deficit. On April 3 Rumsfeld announced: 'The past was not predictable when it started.' On April 14 when Jon Snow asked Clare Short why the UK and USA facilitated the anarchy, she snapped: 'That is not a useful question.' Oh for the plain language of Lord Cornwallis in Wexford 1798: 'Our troops delight in murder.'

My Man of the War Gobbledegook Prize goes to Brigadier General Vincent Brooks of Central Command in Qatar. Asked about the massacre of fourteen civilians on April 7 by the dropping of four two-thousand-pound bombs, Brig Brooks replied 'we are satisfied at the destruction of that facility and with the impacts [sic] we leave'.

For real language, real feeling, I had to cling to Richard Downes, Hilsum, Marlowe, Fisk. On March 26 Downes reported: 'This is war on a terrifying scale.' On April 8 Lindsey Hilsum said: 'Truly this war is awful.' On April 9 Lara Marlowe reported to Pat Kenny: 'It is a criminal thing to shell a hotel.' She was referring to the American shelling of the Palestine Hotel and the killing of journalists about which the Americans told simple, verifiable lies.

Language! What does the phrase 'war criminal' mean? During the British war on Iraq in the 1920s Winston Churchill, then Secretary of State for War and Air, stated: 'I am strongly in favour of using poisoned gas against uncivilised tribes.' Do such sentiments make the Angel of

Dresden a war criminal? What does the word 'democracy' mean? None of the instigators of the invasion of Iraq were elected to office: Rumsfeld, Wolfowitz, Powell, Perle. Seventy-nine billion dollars worth of Boy's Own war!

But now it is the year 2030 and we are in the throes of World War V. China is liberating the USA from the tyranny of George Bush III but, despite the peacemaking efforts of the eighty-eight-year-old Libyan leader of the free world, Colonel Gadaffi, the Chinese armies are making no attempt to keep law and order. Overnight four million prisoners have broken out of their penitentiaries and are joining up with the rest of the populace looting and burning the great cities of America. Veteran RTÉ reporter Richard Downes has described the destruction of every single painting and artefact in the National Gallery in Washington as well the burning down of the Smithsonian Institute. His colleague Mark Little in New York has witnessed the burning down of the New York Public Library, the Met and MoMA. Philip Boucher-Hayes when last heard from was somewhere in Minnesota attempting to escape the clutches of stocious pro-Bush militias. The $60,000 question is: where is George Bush III? The rumour is that he is hiding in the Cuban embassy. However, it is also reported that one of the Bush family jets has been seen landing in Afghanistan. John the Kid Deasy, Prime Minister of Ireland and President of Europe and Arabia, announced from his office in Hungary that the Rule of Law would be upheld and that George Bush III would be required to appear before the international war-crimes tribunal in Dublin Castle. Tomorrow John the Kid Deasy is expected in Baghdad for the Europe and Arabia summit 2030.

April 30, 2003